"Don't be fooled by the title. This is so m   iis
book enjoins the reader on a quest to a d   is
often overlooked by those in academia ar   elf
on a journey of soulful contemplative reflection and examination about my own
drivenness and self-achievement. Tapping the brakes long enough to digest each
chapter allowed time for me to muse about practical ways I could incorporate
more rhythms of play into my own life. This is a helpful tome for the ministry
leader that needs to slow down the cadence of life and find balance. This book
is now tucked in my personal library between the works of Henri Nouwen and
Thomas Merton but it will not remain there long as I will frequent this reference
in my journey toward Christlikeness."

—Michael J. Anthony,
Professor of Educational Ministry & Leadership, Dallas Theological Seminary;
Author of *A Theology for Christian Education*

"I am a better husband, father, and leader because of *A Theology of Play*. Carved
from his own personal experience and biblical wisdom, Kevin paints the clear
directive that Christians should lead the way when it comes to play. Every chapter
can be read as a stand-alone resource to be revisited. God is the author of play,
and Kevin invites us to enjoy life as God intended in the world he created. This
is a must-read for anyone serious about the role of play in our daily lives."

—Joshua Beers,
President, OneLife Institute

"I grew up in a culture that values productivity and frowns upon play. Gushiken's
theological exploration of play makes a strong case for play as a spiritual discipline
and explains play's emotional, relational, vocational, and spiritual benefits. The
book challenges readers to examine barriers to play that distort our view of God
and stop us from enjoying life to the fullest. Read and go play!"

—Ling Dinse, Doctor of Social Work,
Chair of Social Work Department, Messiah University

"In a world which models success through activity and achievement, the idea
of play is not often valued in many global cultures. Refreshing in scope, this
book offers a new construct centered around the practice of play, moving us
to a deeper understanding and practice that play has within our own healthy
spiritual and leadership formations. Thoughtful reflections, practical insights,
and a sound theological basis, provide a tool which could be used for individual
and communal transformation of individuals and the communities they serve."

—Rick Rhoads,
President, BCM International

"As a lifelong Christian and a perfectionist with a loud internal critic, this book is exactly the challenge and permission I needed to let myself learn how to play, and to play more. Play is not only for children, and it's not a sign of immaturity; as Kevin Gushiken points out, it's a mindset that is essential to our faith and growth as followers of Christ at *any* age. I especially needed the chapters on 'Playing in My Identity' and 'Playing at Work' to lighten up aspects of my life that I often take far too seriously. Thanks to Kevin for moving us toward the freedom and pleasure that God intended for our lives through this much-needed book!"

—Angie Ward,
Director of the Doctor of Ministry, Denver Seminary;
Author of *I Am a Leader* and *Uncharted Leadership*

"*A Theology of Play* is a therapeutic solution for the body of Christ. Dr. Gushiken's approach to this book is simplistically deep as he shares from the bowels of his soul. It is apparent that each chapter addresses a layer of his life, while he masterfully mesmerizes his readers through verbal imagery. Dr. Gushiken uses familiar life illustrations that give a reader an affirmation of confidence: the confidence and encouragement that it is all right to play. You will learn about the importance of play. He states that 'Playing involves being present in the moment. It is not possible to truly play if we are thinking about tomorrow.' Dr. Gushiken reminds the reader that barriers may hinder play. If we remove the barriers of hurt and pain, we can experience the freedom God intended. Dr. Gushiken left me with the desire to experience the altruism of play. He states, 'I want to imagine that heaven will be filled with worshiping God, learning about God, communing with God, and playing in the presence of God.'"

—Kevin M. Aiken,
President, Manna Bible Institute;
President of The Cheyney University Foundation;
Lead Pastor, Heart of Worship Restoration Center

"Play, what seemed so simple as a child, becomes more difficult to experience as the years pass. Kevin Gushiken takes the reader on a journey to discover play as God intended us to enjoy. In a biblical, practical, and winsome way, play is introduced back into our hectic lives. Kevin offers insights into play that invite you to discover and consider how it impacts daily life."

—Kevin Oessenich,
Executive Director and CEO, World Team USA

"*A Theology of Play* is not just a book; it's a transformative journey that masterfully intertwines the joy of play with profound theological insights. Kevin's in-depth exploration goes beyond mere analysis, inviting us to discover the divine dance within the realms of play. This book speaks to everyone interested in theology and anyone eager to embrace play as a meaningful and essential part of daily life. It challenges and enriches our understanding, encouraging us to rediscover the liberating power of play. Whether deepening your spiritual journey or seeking more joy in everyday moments, this book is a must-read. Prepare yourself for a compelling journey into the sacred dimensions of laughter, creativity, and connection. It inspires and uplifts the soul, mind, and body, reminding us that play is a human activity and a divine invitation. *A Theology of Play* prompts us to reconsider play's role in our lives, promising personal growth, spiritual enrichment, and an opportunity to play with God in his ongoing creation. This book is a celebration of the spiritual essence of play and a reminder that God is still playing. Join God in this joyful and holy exploration."

—Jorge Barro,
Executive Director, Faculdade Teológica Sul Americana;
Author of *Missional Discipleship*

"Yes for *A Theology of Play*! My background was a conservative local church and Bible college where there was little room for carefree and pleasurable play. 'Don't do a half day's work for the Lord…' was sung. Dr. Gushiken provides a helpful definition and descriptions of 'play,' a strong biblical worldview of the concept, and a thorough discussion with argumentation of why and how play matters. The book is written conversationally, and most titles begin with 'Learning to…' which is an invitation to engage. I believe Dr. Gushiken is the first to provide a fresh and a bold look at the critical role of play in the Christian life."

—Joanna Feliciano-Soberano,
Vice-Chancellor for Academic Affairs, Asian Theological Seminary;
Author of *Teaching Across Cultures*

"Professor and author, Kevin Gushiken, pens a brilliant life-essential that we rarely consider. We are wonderfully awakened to the rhythm and balance that God originally designed. *A Theology of Play* beckons us to a refreshing awareness that gives the reader divine permission to experience life in its abundance and joy to its fullest."

—Wayne Cordeiro,
President and Pastor, New Hope Church and College;
Author of *Leading on Empty* and *The Irresistible Church*

"This book provides a necessary wakeup call to all persons like me, who sometimes are tempted to understand play as the prerogative of children, never as the delight of adulthood. Gushiken effectively debunks that kind of thinking and instead offers a focused apologetic that positions play as our privilege to engage in 'moments in our life as God intended with freedom and presence.' He effectively positions play as an integral part of faithful biblical discipleship rather as an option to consider only when and if we find the time. The chapters are well organized and compelling. I especially valued his focus on unique language of play and his emphasis on the five play languages. Chapter 9, 'Playing at Work,' is worth by itself the price of the book. Overall, this book effectively presents a topic seldom referenced in either leadership or discipleship literature. I highly recommend it!"

— Gene Habecker,
President Emeritus, Taylor University; Senior Fellow, Sagamore Institute;
Author of *The Softer Side of Leadership* and *Rediscovering the Soul of Leadership*

"Finally! A book we in the African church have been waiting for. For a long time, African culture has presented that an unplayful leader is a strong leader—one to be taken seriously. That to play is to lose respect. Pastors and leaders in Africa mostly see playing as contrary to their pious calling and hold stalwartly that 'play' is unspiritual, unserious, for only children, and ultimately of little value. Gushiken has provided thought-provoking and insightful thoughts which ignite a review of Christian expression and hopefully kindles a recapture of play within the rhythms of life. For most of Africa and the world, life is suffering, and Gushiken helpfully shows how to play amid difficulty and pain. Having observed and served leaders in the African space for close to two decades now, I see that Christian leaders must urgently wrestle with how to think about play, and I hope that this guide will furnish conversations on play with its rich biblical and theological perspectives, including how an identity grounded in God's good creation invites us to play, how playing requires permission, how to play in the midst of pain in life, and playing at work. *A Theology of Play* helps break barriers to play in our day-to-day lives no matter our age or culture."

—Richmond Wandera,
President, Pastors Discipleship Network Africa;
Senior Pastor, New Life Baptist Church

A *Theology*
of
Play

LEARNING
TO ENJOY LIFE
AS GOD INTENDED

KEVIN M. GUSHIKEN

KREGEL
ACADEMIC

Published by Kregel Academic, an imprint of Kregel Publications, 2450 Oak Industrial Dr. NE, Grand Rapids, MI 49505-6020.

ISBN 978-0-8254-4865-2

Library of Congress Cataloging-in-Publication Data

Name: Gushiken, Kevin, author.
Title: A theology of play: learning to enjoy life as God intended / by
  Kevin Gushiken.
Description: Grand Rapids, MI: Kregel Academic, [2024] | Includes
  bibliographical references.
Identifiers: LCCN 2023057529 (print) | LCCN 2023057530 (ebook) | ISBN
  9780825448652 (print) | ISBN 9780825473203 (epub) | ISBN 9780825473197
  (kindle)
Subjects: LCSH: Play—Religious aspects—Christianity. | Joy—Religious
  Aspects—Christianity.
Classification: LCC BT709 .G874 2024 (print) | LCC BT709 (ebook) | DDC
  233/.5—dc23/eng/20240207
LC record available at https://lccn.loc.gov/2023057529
LC ebook record available at https://lccn.loc.gov/2023057530

Printed in the United States of America

24 25 26 27 28 / 5 4 3 2 1

To
Penny,
my lifelong playmate

Contents

Acknowledgments 11

Introduction: Let's Begin to Play 13

1. What Is Play? 19

2. Barriers to Play 31

3. Learning to Love Me: Playing in My Identity 43

4. Learning to Be: Playing in the Moment 59

5. Learning to Enjoy Life: Playing Requires Permission 75

6. Learning to Appreciate the World: Playing in Culture 93

7. Learning to Forgive: Playing Involves Removing
   Unnecessary Baggage 111

8. Learning to Live in Freedom: Playing Involves Putting
   Aside Guilt and Shame 125

9. Learning to Lighten Up: Playing at Work 137

10. Learning to Embrace Discomfort: Playing in the Pain of Life 153

Epilogue: Learning to Hope: Playing in Glory 167

Bibliography 171

Acknowledgments

To Jesus—my Savior, my Lord, and my friend—I am eternally grateful. Without salvation, it would be impossible for me to enjoy life, let alone play. I am thankful that I am a child of the Living God, secure and content, which is the essence of the abundant life.

To my wife, Penny, words are not adequate. You are my biggest supporter. You are my dearest friend. I cannot imagine life without you. You have been a conversation partner during brainstorming sessions. You helped fine-tune this work by attentively editing the manuscript. And life with you has provided the foundation to speak on the topic of play. May we richly play until God calls us home.

To Ashleigh and Ryan, who constantly tease me about my need to play, I am so privileged to be your dad. I have learned so much about enjoying life through our daily playful interactions, intense seize-the-day vacations, and memories on Lake Michigan sailing or on a Lancaster field throwing the ball. It is a joy to now see you grab hold of life as adults. May you have a life filled with play.

To my mom, for her constant support over the years. When I first received the contract, you immediately told friends (and even strangers). You have always demonstrated a motherly pride. It is a joy to now have you living near us so that we can play as a family more regularly.

To Kregel, thank you for your constant support during this project. I appreciate you taking a chance on the proposal and making my thoughts become a reality. I am specifically grateful for Robert Hand, Kevin McKissick, Bethany Murphy, and Shawn Vander Lugt. Your assistance during every step of this journey has been a rich blessing.

INTRODUCTION

Let's Begin to Play

We don't stop playing because we grow old; we grow old because we stop playing.
— George Bernard Shaw

This book is about play. It is my hope that the contents of this book will inspire you to enjoy life more fully, with exuberance and richness. It is my prayer that your life will gradually be marked with regular moments and seasons of play. I would love nothing more than to hear that play has become a natural part of your life without scheduling it— spontaneous play. Imagine that: play just happening in your life.

There has been tremendous research on the science of play. In 2010, Stuart Brown wrote the national best-selling book *Play*. It is an incredible work that unpacks research on how play impacts us intellectually and emotionally. He is also the founder of the National Institute for Play, a nonprofit organization committed to the promotion of play. Jaak Panksepp wrote in *The Archaeology of Mind*, "A rigorous scientific approach to play reveals that all mammals possess a fundamental brain system, PLAY, which accounts for the universal inclination to play. Current research suggests that the PLAY system may be especially important in the epigenetic development and maturation of the neocortex" (Panksepp and Rivin 2012, 386).

Further, research has shown that play is connected to healthy human development. For children, playing unlocks creativity that encourages self-discovery (Winnicott 1971). It is proven to aid in the healing of children who have experienced abuse, which has spawned play therapy to help restore emotional well-being (Cattanach 1993). Play benefits not only in the immediate but also over the long term. It can enhance a person's health years later (Frost 2010). Studies have shown that the absence of play has led to significant emotional issues later in life. Stuart Brown stated,

> Sustained, moderate to severe play deprivation particularly during the first 10 years of life appeared linked to major varied but virtually omnipresent emotional dysregulation; i.e., increased prevalence of depression, a tendency to become mired in rigid inflexible perceptions of options available for adaptation, diminished impulse control, less self regulation, increased addictive predilection, diminished management of aggression, and fragility and shallowness of enduring interpersonal relationships. (Brown 2014)

In essence, play is essential for emotional health, and the absence of play leads to depression, moodiness, and narcissism (Brown 2014).

Play not only impacts the individual but also improves social welfare. Joe Frost, in *A History of Children's Play and Play Environments*, detailed how the "diminution, modification, and/or disappearance of play" in modern culture is negatively impacting social welfare (2009). Play is good for our relationships and societal interactions. It allows us to engage with others in an emotionally healthy manner. We are hardwired to play. Play activates the frontal cortex. In fact, affective neuroscientists have proven that humans are born with seven primary-process emotional systems, one being play (Narvaez 2012). We are created to play, individually and with one another. It has personal and societal benefits.

This raises a primary concern of this book. If scientists affirm the benefits of play, should not also theologians? More specifically, should not Christians who know and worship the creator of all truth, theological and scientific, affirm and embrace play? It is my conviction that God designed humans with the capacity to play. He desires that we engage in play for personal pleasure, community enrichment, and spiritual expression.

Play is a gift given to us by God. That is why I titled this book *A Theology of Play*. This book is meant to provide a theological treatment of play for the purposes of grounding play in a Christian worldview. It is from this perspective that one can embrace play in the mindset and manner intended by God. As will be presented in this book, I believe Christians should lead the charge on play. We should celebrate, enjoy, and honor God through it. As such, if you have not yet received Christ, I encourage you to seriously consider doing so as you read this book. While play is God's gift to humanity, a relationship with Jesus will enable you to experience the fullness of play as designed and desired by God.

This book is divided into ten chapters. Each chapter contains a different focus, ranging from work to forgiveness. Chapter 1, "What is Play?," unpacks the definition of play. It explores the biblical foundations of play, including the key verses supporting the topic. It also introduces an overarching theological framework for play. In sum, the overall rationale for a biblical exploration of play is developed to provide a foundation for the book.

Prior to developing a construct of play, it is necessary to unpack those things that hold us back from play. Chapter 2, "Barriers to Play," discusses some of these obstacles, including seriousness, discontentment, resentment, time commitments, unbalanced theology, personal backgrounds, and division. Specific application to the church is provided. This chapter might require some pausing as you think of your own roadblocks to play, and I encourage you to take time to do so.

The next chapter, "Learning to Love Me: Playing in My Identity," unpacks personal identity and how it is shaped by historic and societal influences. In contrast, Christians are to be framed by God's perspective of them—they are to have a God-identity. The relationship between identity and play is woven throughout the chapter. We will center on two specific applications to identity and play: appearance and personality. Personally, this is one of my favorite chapters.

Chapter 4 is titled "Learning to Be: Playing in the Moment." We are oftentimes bound to the past or focused on the future, which prevents us from being in the moment, a necessity for play. This chapter unravels the primary theological reasons as to why it is challenging to live in the moment. Practical application as to how to begin "being" in the realm of play is discussed. For me, this chapter is the hardest to live out. I am a planner; therefore, it is hard to be in the moment. If the same is true for you, strap in for this chapter, as it might be uncomfortable.

The next chapter is "Learning to Enjoy Life: Playing Requires Permission." Life has become very serious. We are conditioned to prioritize duty and obligation, both at work and home. As a result, play can be neglected because we feel irresponsible when we enjoy moments of life. It is thus necessary to give ourselves permission. This is a novel idea—needing permission to play. Yet, when we think about it, it makes sense. This chapter unpacks how to create personal allowance and space for play.

As a Westerner, it is tempting to frame play simply through my cultural context. Yet this would be a mistake, particularly in developing a theology of play. To appreciate the beauty of God's multicultural world, it is essential to consider cultural particularities of play. While it is impossible to look exhaustively at culture, chapter 6, "Learning to Appreciate the World: Playing in Culture," strives to acknowledge the unique role culture has in the topic of play.

At times, it is necessary to look backward in order to move forward. Chapter 7, "Learning to Forgive: Playing Involves Removing Unnecessary Baggage," unearths a difficult but necessary topic for play. Hurt suffocates play. Oftentimes, we are unable to play because we are holding on to the baggage of pain and resentment. As a result, we live in the past. This chapter explores forgiveness, of self and others, as a necessary step toward play. I pray that you experience true freedom as you work through this chapter.

We live in a world of guilt and shame. We experience regrets and embarrassments. These can pile up, resulting in bondage. Chapter 8 is titled "Learning to Live in Freedom: Playing Involves Putting Aside Guilt and Shame." Freedom is often misunderstood in society. This chapter explores the biblical concept of freedom and how it connects to one's ability to play. The notions of shame and false guilt are discussed from a biblical perspective. If you are battling with these issues, I pray that you find peace through reading this chapter.

To truly experience play, it is necessary for it to touch every aspect of our lives. Today's work environment is rigid, demanding, and at times oppressive, and yet research indicates that individuals who enjoy work are more productive. The next chapter, "Learning to Lighten Up: Playing at Work," explores the benefits of play at work, not only in terms of vocational enjoyment but also work productivity. Play has the unique power to enrich one's job while also improving mental health—key concerns in today's work environments. This chapter is designed for both the employer and the employee.

The true test of a theology of play is if it is applicable to the darkest moments of life. The final chapter, "Learning to Embrace Discomfort: Playing in the Pain of Life," explores how it is often assumed that play is only possible when life is good. But to truly play it is essential to create space for play in the midst of difficulties. This chapter discusses pain from a theological perspective and how, rather than preventing us from playing, pain highlights the necessity of even more play. This chapter was deeply personal for me. I hope that anyone undergoing painful difficulties finds comfort and hope in this chapter.

I wrestled as to whether to include eleven chapters by adding one on heaven. I chose instead to have the epilogue focus on this topic. It seemed like an appropriate section to follow the chapter on pain, as well as a fitting end to the book. The epilogue is titled "Learning to Hope: Playing in Glory." The Bible is largely silent about life in heaven. We know we will worship God. We know that our lives will be fully sanctified. We know that pain will cease to exist. I also believe that we will fully enjoy the experience, including moments of play. This epilogue inspires great anticipation for me as I look beyond this life. I hope it does for you as well.

I indicated that the first chapter lays a biblical foundation for play. Even though numerous verses are covered in this chapter, it does not comprise the summation of this book's theological treatment. Each chapter is filled with rich theology and Bible verses. This is intentional, in order to provide a foundation for each chapter so as to present a theology that is deeply integrated and holistic.

I bathed this book deeply in prayer. I strived to faithfully honor the Word of God. As an inerrantist, I poured over each biblical reference to ensure it reflected the true intent of the passage. I did not want to force a passage into saying something that would be even remotely misaligned. I consulted theologians and commentaries to ensure theological accuracy. And I desired to allow the text to breathe by offering a plain reading of the passages. Numerous times I wrestled over a specific word to ensure theological integrity. I understand that some might disagree with the interpretations of certain texts. However, I request that you approach this book with an open mind to its theological importance, relevance, and application to play. My prayer is that this book might offer you a different perspective on God's desire for us as his beloved creation.

To gain the most out of this book, I recommend digesting each chapter slowly. Rather than sitting down and reading the book in one sitting, take your time. Grab a cup of coffee and read through its contents leisurely and intentionally. Mull them over. You will find this book at times philosophical and other times practical. Most of all, I pray you find it helpful. Reflect on your life and your aspirations. Strive to discover the reasons that prevent you from playing so that you can step into play. View this book as a potential game changer in your life. If you want to pause and implement a particular chapter into your life before moving on to the next one, go for it. The end goal is to cultivate a lifestyle of play rather than complete the book. To do so requires time and space. To assist you, each chapter concludes with some reflection questions and helpful recommendations. I encourage you to take time to read through these practical considerations. They are designed to wrap up each chapter and move its contents into your life. Some of you process better in community. If that is you, find some friends and read the book together. This can serve as mutual encouragement and accountability. When finished, hand it off to someone else. If it blesses you, perhaps it might bless others. Lastly, enjoy this book. Have fun with it. And, most of all, begin to play!

CHAPTER 1

What Is Play?

The true object of all human life is play.
                                        —G. K. Chesterton

Can you remember a time when you truly played? Can you picture the scene? I can. It was 2011. It was a perfect August day in Chicago. I was on a thirty-six-foot sailboat with my family. We had just raised the sails. The wind was blowing from the northwest at approximately ten knots. The sun was shining brightly, warming the sides of our faces. The sails were fully stretched with a small hint of luffing. We could hear seagulls on a breakwater as we left the harbor. The sound of the city grew fainter as we headed east toward open water with only a few boats in sight. We were laughing and smiling as the wind gently whipped through our hair. My son was enjoying the winches on the boat. My wife stretched out her legs in the boat's cockpit. I handed the wheel to my daughter and she guided us into the large expanse of Lake Michigan.

I felt free. I had no care in the world. I was in the moment. I was living life to the fullest. It seemed as if time had stopped. If someone had photographed that moment, I would have had a smile stretched across my face. Life seemed rich and full. It was an experience I wished would never have to end. Even now, I am smiling thinking about the emotions of being free to simply let go and play. Can you recall your own moment?

What if these moments were not nostalgic experiences but regular parts of our lives? What if we were able to harness this perspective so it not only characterized an event but became embedded into our attitude in life? What if play became a part of our daily lives, like drinking coffee or combing our hair? Would it not revolutionize our lives?

PLAY DEFINED

Play is a word easily recognizable but defined differently depending on the person and the context. I could poll one hundred persons regarding their definitions of *play*, and I would likely get one hundred different responses. For some, it is defined in the context of sports, such as playing football or soccer. For others, it is a theatrical performance: "I went to a musical play." For many, it is what occurs during an activity, "I went bowling and just played for the evening."

The English language is complicated. We can use the same word in different ways, and it captures an entirely different meaning. In the case of *play*, it can be a noun or a verb. It can be an activity or the action within that activity. *Play* can also be used as an adjective, as in "Dancing is a playful activity." For most people, the play that is most attractive involves spontaneous, leisurely moments in life when you experience life to the fullest. It involves the experience of freedom and joy in loving a moment in life.

In this book, I want to propose that we see play as a characteristic of our lives rather than separate from our lives, regardless of whether it is a noun, verb, or adjective. I want us to embrace a lifestyle of play, a mindset of play. I want play to infuse our being so that it changes how we see life.

As a Christian, I am defining play as *the God-given ability and permission to fully enjoy moments in life as God intended, with freedom and pleasure.* Jesus said, "I came that they may have life and have it abundantly" (John 10:10). This passage is appropriately understood as involving the spiritual realm—that we are to find fullness of life in redemption. However, I believe Jesus has a more holistic perspective in mind—that we, in all aspects of life, can enjoy life abundantly, viewing all life as spiritual, since we are made in God's image and living in God's world. Thus, an abundant life involves contentment in God's physical blessings. It consists of joy in using the gifts and abilities God has given to us. It embodies thankfulness that as created beings we have the capacity to love another person. Yet it should also involve play—moments to fully and leisurely celebrate life.

For context, in the next verse, Jesus describes himself as the "good shepherd." Certainly, our Good Shepherd desires that we enjoy his good world. Play is an expression of this enjoyment—a life perspective that seeks to enjoy the everyday moments of life.

CONFESSION

I need to confess something immediately in the opening pages of this book. The book is not simply for others; it is for me. I am a perfectionist. In fact, I like to perfect perfectionism. There are type A people. My son jokes that I am a triple-A battery. As a result, I am highly driven. I am always setting goals. I am striving to excel in all areas—vocationally and personally. Even a simple pleasure such as jogging can easily turn into a competition with myself. I desire to improve my time every time I run, to the precise second. When I miss the mark, there is some disappointment. Fellow perfectionists are nodding their heads in agreement; non-perfectionists are perplexed, saying, "Just enjoy the run!"

There are some people who are past-driven. They are always looking backward at mistakes or regrets. That is not me. I tend to live by the mantra carpe diem, or "seize the day." For me, ambition is my primary barrier to play.

Personally, I need this book. I need to think more deeply about play. I need to wrestle with the things in my life that prevent me from playing. I need to embody a more playful attitude. In some respects, I hope this book is therapeutic for me. I hope I can begin to practice the very thing that I long for—to play.

WHAT DOES THE BIBLE SAY ABOUT PLAY?

There are few references to play in the Bible. In each case, they describe an act. And they each involve children and animals. The passages involving children are Job 41:5 and Matthew 11:16–17. Job 41:5 asks, "Will you play with him as with a bird, or will you put him on a leash for your girls?" This verse references Leviathan, asking whether one can play with such a formidable creature. Matthew 11:16–17 states, "But to what shall I compare this generation? It is like children sitting in the marketplaces and calling to their playmates, 'We played the flute for you, and you did not dance; we sang a dirge, and you did not mourn.'"

The primary purpose of these verses in Matthew is to unpack a spiritual truth—the fickleness of religious leaders to dismiss John the Baptist and Jesus. I recognize this intent. However, in both Matthew and Job, play is viewed as morally neutral. In the first reference, it is a leisure exchange; in the second passage, it captures a skillful act—to successfully produce music using an instrument. In each case, there is nothing wrong with the act of playing. John Nolland, in his commentary on Matthew, stated, "It is clear that the playing of the flute is an invitation to dance, perhaps at a wedding" (2005, 461). Affirmed in these verses is a liberating truth: play is a normal aspect of life affirmed in Scripture.

There are two references in the Bible to animals playing. Psalm 104:25–26 states,

> Here is the sea, great and wide,
> which teems with creatures innumerable,
> living things both small and great.
> There go the ships,
> and Leviathan, which you formed to play in it.

Job 40:20 references the arena for Behemoth by stating, "For the mountains yield food for him where all the wild beasts play." Like the passages related to children, playing in the sea and in the mountains are viewed as morally neutral forms of pleasure. The passages describe leisure in the natural order. Both children and animals are described as playing in God's world.

If children and animals are permitted to play, why not adults? If children are described as participating in play in a way that is natural and amoral, should not adults equally be permitted to do so? Adults are no less human than children. Yet, why is it that play sometimes stops once we reach adulthood?

Implied Passages of Play

In addition to direct references to play, I would argue that the idea of play is implied throughout Scripture. The purpose of Scripture is not to be exhaustive but rather to present the essential record of God's story and the requisite instruction and teaching necessary to live a Christ-centered, gospel-informed, fulfilled life. It would be a mistake to exclude certain aspects of life simply because they are not recorded in Scripture. For example, Scripture does not discuss vacationing, yet it is an acceptable, embraced part of life. For me, play lands in this space. It is an implied reality in Scripture.

Ecclesiastes 3:1 states, "For everything there is a season, and a time for every matter under heaven." One of the times described is laughing and dancing: "a time to weep, and a time to *laugh*; a time to mourn, and a time to *dance*" (3:4). Scripture explicitly records that we should laugh, and we should dance. In his work on Ecclesiastes, J. Stafford Wright stated, "A Christian should not be perpetually facetious, but neither should he avoid occasions of social happiness" (1991, 1161). To this, I say a hearty "Amen."

Laughing and dancing sound a lot like play to me!

The Old Testament

In the Old Testament, the Israelites were instructed to celebrate feasts and festivals. These events had specific spiritual intents and instructions. However, they were also times in the year when Jews could break from work, reflect on Yahweh, and simply be. Yes, there were offerings and spiritual tasks to be conducted; however, these events consisted of times to celebrate with others in the community.

Leviticus 23 introduces the primary Jewish feasts. Verses 1–2 state, "The LORD spoke to Moses, saying, 'Speak to the people of Israel and say to them, These are the appointed feasts of the LORD that you shall proclaim as holy convocations; they are my appointed feasts.'" Laird Harris, in his commentary, stated that the word *feasts* "is misleading" (1990, 622). The phrase "set celebrations" might be better (Harris 1990, 622). The rationale is that these events were not simply meals but times of celebration. Celebration in the Old Testament involved more than food; it included singing and playing instruments. They were moments to rejoice in God's work.

When I hear Christians discuss the Israelite feasts and festivals, it is typically with the goal of understanding the spiritual significance of them, particularly how they point to Christ. This should be the primary task for

Christians. However, is it not also helpful to see the day-to-day living that occurred in the midst of the feasts and festivals and apart from the offerings and religious tasks? There certainly were playful moments between the formal religious activities. These occasions were opportunities for God's people to be present in community, apart from work, for the purpose of enjoying God's gift of life, provision, and redemption. This is helpful instruction to us when we see these passages in their lived realities. People loved life. They celebrated God's work. They fellowshipped around meals. They were certainly *enjoying life as God intended, with freedom and pleasure.* I believe one reason God commanded feasts and festivals throughout the year was to force people to break, rest, and enjoy life. Apart from clear instruction to do so, humans are prone to follow routine. And routine becomes the breeding ground for the mundane—a life of duty without play.

The New Testament

In John 2:1–12, we see Jesus attending a wedding. During this wedding, Jesus performed one of his first miracles when he turned water into wine, typically understood as the first sign of his divinity in John's gospel. It is a marvelous scene. It is a passage where his divine nature is illustrated. Most certainly, this is the primary purpose of these verses in John's gospel. Yet we should not overlook the context of verses 1–2: "On the third day there was a wedding at Cana in Galilee, and the mother of Jesus was there. Jesus also was invited to the wedding with his disciples." There was a wedding with celebration, food, and certainly dancing. Individuals were at play. And Jesus was present. I imagine he enjoyed himself at the wedding. After all, he encouraged the celebration by making wine from water. A careful reading of the passage highlights that the only individuals who knew Jesus performed the miracle were his mother, the disciples, and the servants. Jesus did not broadcast the miracle. In the moment, he performed this act so that others could continue enjoying the wedding. He was encouraging the celebration. He endorsed this moment of play.

Spiritually Integrated Play

Second Samuel 6:16 states, "As the ark of the LORD came into the city of David, Michal the daughter of Saul looked out of the window and saw King David leaping and dancing before the LORD, and she despised him in her heart." This activity was a spiritual moment of worship. David made offerings to the Lord and celebrated God's sovereignty and goodness. And, in this act, in the presence of the ark, David leaped and danced. David experienced pleasure. And God was pleased. Dance in this passage is clearly connected to a spiritual moment of worship. It was not simply a leisure event.

For some theologians, this passage endorses vibrant worship—meaning individuals should dance and leap, but only within the confines of worship. I would like to broaden our understanding of worship. In the Old Testament, worship was largely confined to a locale. People traveled for certain festivals, such as the Day of Atonement, because worship was linked to the presence of the Lord. And, since God dwelled in the temple, individuals traveled to its location to worship. The temple of God resided in a place.

In the New Testament, the temple no longer resides in a place; it is in persons. Paul wrote, "Or do you not know that your body is a temple of the Holy Spirit within you, whom you have from God? You are not your own, for you were bought with a price. So glorify God in your body" (1 Cor. 6:19–20). The temple is no longer stationary in a location; it is embodied in humans. We are mobile temples. The presence of God resides in us as his individual arks. This truth communicates the liberating power of the gospel—the incarnational nature of God's presence in humans through the Holy Spirit.

As Christians, we are to embody Christ in all aspects of life. Paul wrote in that passage that we are to glorify God with our bodies. Later in 1 Corinthians, Paul wrote, "So, whether you eat or drink, or whatever you do, do all to the glory of God" (10:31). Glorifying God is not relegated to dedicated spiritual acts such as worship, Bible reading, or church attendance. It involves every aspect of our lives, including eating and drinking. For me, these verses articulate a powerful truth. We are to worship God always, on every occasion, because we are temples of God—dwellings for the Holy Spirit. If this is true, every aspect of life should be worshipful. Worship should then be evident in community gatherings, such as church, Bible studies, and fellowship, and also in family and individual moments, such as vacations, dinners, teaching moments, leisure activities, and even chores. Worship is thus a state of being, not an act.

To draw inference from David, if God was pleased with David's worship, which included dancing, should not our everyday, common-place moments of worship also allow for dancing? And, if dancing is an expression of play, cannot our play be worshipful to God, not in a formal sense but as leisure moments when we celebrate life? What I am arguing for is a view that sees play not as isolated from spirituality but as an expression of spirituality, like eating and drinking, as Paul said. Play can be worshipful in that it expresses our delight with God by living the abundant life in all aspects. In this sense, worship and play, while at times explicitly and expressly focused on celebrating God's nature, can also be embodied in the natural rhythms of life when we are conscious of God but not necessarily verbally declaring him.

PLAY REDEEMED

Play is not uniquely Christian. It is a human reality. Yet play can be re-deemed by Christians. I have stated that play is morally neutral. However, that does not mean play does not have moral expressions. An individual can be "playing" during a game of soccer but do so competitively and selfishly. In this sense, play becomes all about the individual. In other cases, a person "plays" while attending a party, only to find themselves getting drunk. This expression of play is immoral. An individual can also have a carefree mentality whereby their focus is on enjoying life—"I just want to play." If prolonged, this attitude of play can neglect human responsibilities of duty and family. In these instances, play is perhaps an escape from reality.

While play is morally neutral, it finds worshipful expression when it is within the parameters of moral living. In this sense, we become gen-uinely human by living the life God intended for us. Play in this regard is truly free, not by escaping reality but by embracing true reality—the life God intended for us, one of righteousness and holiness. By fully em-bracing Christ, we are free to live in freedom and pleasure. And, when we understand that life is to be enjoyed in all its wonders, play becomes permissible and life-giving.

Play is also a vehicle for celebration. When something good happens in life, we want to express it through leisure. We want to go have fun and enjoy the moment. It is an opportunity to live and smile. As Christians, we are redeemed. We have been delivered from sin. Christ has rescued us. An eternal home awaits us. Should we not play in beautiful and celebratory ways in response to God's work in our lives? Furthermore, should not Christians be the most playful, since we can play as God intended? Play for Christians is not an escape from the challenges of life but an attitude of celebration, even in the midst of life's difficulties. Play is not carefree living but purposeful enjoyment of life.

Play gives us pleasure, but it also gives God pleasure. God delights when we live as he intended, including moments of play. If play is a part of being human in this world—an expression of leisure and an attitude of enjoyment, should not Christians be the first to embrace play? Should we not play as a means of worship as image bearers of God? Should we not model play to the world in a way that is freeing and life-giving? Should we not celebrate play in others rather than stifle it? In other words, why should non-Christians have the most "fun" when in fact God infused play into the fabric of life? Since we know the Creator and Author of play, we are at an advantage in that we can play as God desires—with freedom and pleasure, living life abundantly.

As I write this chapter, my son has just finished an intense season. He completed his junior year of high school, which involved taking three AP exams and the SAT. In addition to the rigors of preparing for these tests during school, he also studied at home, using various preparatory books. During this time, he also competed on the track team, attended prom, participated in his youth group and small groups, practiced karate, and worked part time. It was not uncommon during this two-month stretch for him to get five hours of sleep. There were days when he was exhausted and frustrated at the pace of life. During this season, he longed for a moment of play—to go enjoy life without demands and responsibilities. He wanted to just live in the moment, not for some future test or obligation. He wanted to be free to laugh and joke. As his parents, we were proud of his work ethic and commitment to success in school and life. And because we deeply love him, we also wanted him to enjoy life.

So we encouraged him on numerous occasions to take a break and "go play." We would tell him to go hang out with his friends, enjoy a movie, or grab something to eat with his youth group. These moments were life-giving because they allowed him to be free and spontaneous, even briefly, from life's responsibilities. They were not an escape from reality, as mentioned above, because he wanted to work hard, but rather they were a simple reprieve to enjoy life. We love him and so we wanted him to play because it invigorated him. It was both good and necessary for his management of life.

God loves us. He sees the demands and responsibilities of life. He knows that we have duties and obligations—to work and to family. He recognizes that life is difficult and hard because of sin. He knows that at times we are holding on by a thread, feeling frustrated, exasperated, and overwhelmed. Because he loves us, he not only permits play but wants us to play. He desires for us to be free and spontaneous, even briefly, from life's responsibilities. He recognizes that it is both good and necessary for us. Play is a means by which God provides a life-giving oasis in the desert moments of life.

WHY THE WORD *PLAY*

You might be asking, why are you choosing the word *play*. Would it not be more biblically accurate to use the word *joy* instead of *play*? For me, joy is a feeling of pleasure based on our identity and salvation in Christ. We have joy because of who we are in Christ. In this sense, it is largely attached to the truth that we are new creations in Christ (2 Cor. 5:17). It is directly connected to our relationship with God.

Play, on the other hand, is being defined as *the God-given ability and permission to fully enjoy moments in life as God intended, with freedom and pleasure*. It involves the horizontal plane as residents in this world. It is a way of approaching life that is celebratory and natural. It is a manner by which we affirm our security in Christ that then allows us to be present in the moment. It is permission to enjoy the goodness of God within his good world.

And truthfully, I chose *play* because it vividly captures something that we long for in life. Who does not want to play? Who does not want to let go and live a little? Who does not get to the end of a busy week and say, "I just want to go play"? For me, I want to play in life. I want to be more playful. It is incredibly enticing. For me, I miss being a child, the time when I could be in the moment and laugh. I believe this joy is God's desire for us. It is not simply a component of childhood. It is an aspect of life. Play sounds so appealing to me. So I am choosing *play* to help us recapture how we can see life. Is it the most biblically accurate word? Possibly not. But it does visually capture something that is deeply missing in the church and among Christians.

SUMMARIZING THOUGHTS

Christian apologist G. K. Chesterton wrote,

> It is not only possible to say a great deal in praise of play; it is really possible to say the highest things in praise of it. It might reasonably be maintained that the true object of all human life is play. Earth is a task garden; heaven is a playground. To be at last in such secure innocence that one can juggle with the universe and the stars, to be so good that one can treat everything as a joke—that may be, perhaps, the real end and final holiday of human souls. (2009, 35)

In essence, we oftentimes view the real action as eventually taking place in heaven. As such, we view earth as a time of waiting for that eventual consummation. As a result, this earthly life becomes very serious, a "task garden," rather than a time to inaugurate a bit of that "heavenly playground" in this world—a taste of our "real end and final holiday." God desires that we play in the here and now. It is a gift for us as his beloved creations. It is a way to celebrate this glorious life that he has given to us. And by enjoying this gift, it is a means to honor him as our benevolent God and Creator.

REFLECTION

To reimagine our lives around play requires reflection. Our definition of play has likely been framed around activities or leisure, or it is an aspect of our distance past—childhood. For others, it is something that seems impossible due to our hectic, stressful lives. Thinking of play as an ongoing aspect of life requires focus, attention, and reorientation. It involves believing that God permits and desires for his children to play.

I encourage you to take time to mull over the following questions and then respond honestly. Allow yourself to move toward an attitude of play. Be patient with yourself, as life reorientation takes time. But begin the process of *enjoying life as God intended.*

1. Think about a moment when you truly played. What were you doing? What did you feel? How did you see life?

2. When you think of play, what comes to mind? What characterizes an experience of play?

3. Do you believe God gives you permission to play? Why or why not?

4. What is preventing you from seeing play as an act of worship?

5. What is one thing you can do to begin moving toward an attitude of play?

CHAPTER 2

Barriers to Play

To me, there are three things we all should do every day. Number one is laugh. You should laugh every day. Number two is think, we should spend some time in thought. And number three is you should have your emotions moved to tears.

—Jimmy Valvano

The famed basketball coach Jimmy Valvano shared the above words in 1993 during a speech at the ESPY Awards ceremony, two months prior to his passing from adenocarcinomatous cancer. If I were to embrace these three things, it would indeed revolutionize my life. In thinking about these three things, I would add a fourth one—play. A full life is one in which a person plays.

As I write these words, the world is emerging from a two-year pandemic. This period has been an incredibly depressing one. We have been limited in our movements. Mask mandates have been the norm. Racial tensions have erupted in different parts of the world. In the United States, politics have been polarizing. The images of Ukraine have haunted us. It seems there has been very little to celebrate, let alone reason to play.

I suspect you are like me in that you simply hoped to survive this time. Month by month, you went through the motions, tracking current

COVID-19 levels with the hope that you could enjoy some freedom. You celebrated when the cases were low by venturing out and enjoying life again, even if only for a moment. Yet these hopes were dashed when the cases rose. If you were like me, you were attaching leisure, or one's ability to play, to whether the virus situation had improved or not. In doing so, we were *linking play to external circumstances*. Perhaps this is one reason we were not able to play. It is dependent on ideal conditions. Yet play should not be conditional to something outside of us; it should be possible regardless of the circumstances.

THE CHURCH

I am writing this book for the church. As a Christian, I have recently wondered why the church has a unique capacity to suppress joy. I joke with my kids that it seems like the church at times is looking around for enjoyment, and, if they see it, they say, "Happiness. We can't have that. We need to deal with it. Let's stomp on it!" For some, a committee might even be formed to investigate the happiness to see if it aligns with our doctrinal statements—to see if it should be allowed.

To be fair, I don't think the church intentionally squashes play. We want people to be happy; however, when push comes to shove, seriousness takes over. In recent years, it seems the church has become way too serious. We define our existence based on what we are against in this world. Equally, we are never satisfied with our spiritual walk and are always encouraging further discipleship and growth. In many respects, being a good Christian is becoming defined by what we do and how we look rather than who we are.

I am becoming increasingly convinced that play should be part of our discipleship process. I believe it might revolutionize our love for God, our lives, and each other if we asked one another, "Have you played this week? Have you truly enjoyed a moment where you smiled and laughed and enjoyed life?" Oh, I think we would love it. The problem is not our desire for such an existence. Rather, it is that we do not give ourselves permission to play. We feel guilty if we play, believing falsely that we should be doing something serious or productive. Perhaps we should begin to see play as an aspect of being productive.

Christians, of all people, should truly play because God declares certain amazing truths about us. The following are a few of these promises for us to reflect upon.

- We are loved by our heavenly Father. Jeremiah recorded God stating, "I have loved you with an everlasting love" (Jer. 31:3).
- We have the capacity to truly forgive and be forgiven. Paul stated, "Be kind to one another, tenderhearted, forgiving one another, as God in Christ forgave you" (Eph. 4:32).
- We can live a life of purpose. A psalmist stated, "I cry out to God Most High, to God who fulfills his purpose for me" (Ps. 57:2).
- We have the promise of an amazing future. Jesus stated, "In my Father's house are many rooms. If it were not so, would I have told you that I go to prepare a place for you? And if I go and prepare a place for you, I will come again and will take you to myself, that where I am you may be also" (John 14:2–3).

Considering these truths, we should live life to the fullest, *playfully*. We should enjoy life abundantly in light of these realities.

Granted, I am not calling for an abolishment of responsibility. It is necessary to be serious at times. I need to work. I need to pay my bills. I need to make decisions in life. I need to wrestle with difficult issues, including broken relationships and health diagnoses. I need to weep at the sight of horrific injustices around the world. Yes, there is a season for everything. Yet we somehow have deleted Ecclesiastes 3:4—there is "a time to dance"—from our Bibles. No, this is not a call for samba lessons (although that would not be a bad thing). It is a call for us to dance in life. It is call for us to play.

BARRIERS TO PLAY

It is tempting to think about the idea of play and simply respond with action. I need to have a hobby. I need to chill out more. I need to watch funny videos so I can laugh. I need to take more vacations. I need to get out and enjoy a day to myself. However, to do so would be to frame play around activities. I think play goes much deeper. To play involves a reorientation toward life. It involves us seeing God's world and ourselves differently. I do not want you to walk away from this book with a list of to-dos. If this were the takeaway for you, I would have failed miserably. I want you to be different; I want to be different.

In the next few pages, I would like to articulate several barriers to play. This is not an exhaustive list. You could certainly come up with additional ones. However, it frames a list that I see as primary attitudes and realities that suppress play and even prevent us from playing. I hope you will take time to reflect on these barriers. I encourage you not to race through these barriers but rather sit with them. They might help you begin to diagnose why you are not able to play.

Barrier 1: Seriousness

I discussed this barrier in the section on the church. But the blame does not lie with the church; it lies with us. We are the ones that embrace seriousness. Perhaps we don't intentionally do so; however, it can easily permeate the fabric of our lives. Perhaps this routine sounds familiar to you: You wake up. Then you go to work. After work, you attend to family responsibilities and exercise. After you have completed your daily responsibilities, you retreat to a show or a movie for a few minutes before going to bed. The next day, you rinse and repeat. The weekend involves getting caught up with anything missed during the week, including chores and bills. On Sunday, you attend church. Emerging from church, you might leave with some important takeaways that you need to implement in your spiritual life. You then prepare for another week.

You might have moments of play scattered throughout the week by smelling the roses or inviting friends over for a game night. You might plan a vacation and dream of the places you will see. Certainly, there are moments of play. But they are scheduled. They are isolated. They are moments of leisure. I am arguing for an attitude of *playfulness* that encompasses our entire day. Unfortunately, life has become way too serious. And that seriousness kills play.

Barrier 2: Discontentment

Connected to seriousness is discontentment. Discontentment is grounded in the attitude of restlessness. It is a belief that one is not satisfied or, like I've experienced at times, that one cannot be satisfied. It fails to see and affirm God's blessings in our lives. It lives for improvement. At times, there is a high that is produced in striving for something more. Mistakenly, we sometimes believe that contentment can be found if we achieve or obtain enough. However, the true source of the problem—a need to improve—will not change once things are achieved or obtained. The internal cause of discontentment will continue driving us forward to the next thing.

The reason discontentment is a barrier to play is that it always focuses on what is missing rather than what one already has. To play, you need to *like* life. You might not love it because of your circumstances, but you do need to like it. If you are discontent, why would you want to celebrate it? And how could you play if the things you have in life are not enjoyable? To use a childhood example, if a child does not like the toy, she will not play with the toy. If we do not like our lives, we will not play in the midst of life.

Barrier 3: Resentment

Resentment is backward looking. It is fixated on a past hurt or slight in one's life. It typically involves pain received from a loved one. But it can also involve societal woes. I know several people who are resentful over poor treatment by an organization or church. For others, it might involve being the victim of discrimination or abuse. In no way am I advocating for dismissing these hurts as illegitimate. They are legitimate. They are serious concerns. And they demand a response, perhaps even through confrontation.

However, there is a difference between recognizing the need for justice and resentment. Justice is acting upon a personal or societal wrong in a way that speaks truth into a situation and strives for societal reform. Christians are called to justice. Micah 6:8 states, "He has told you, O man, what is good; and what does the LORD require of you but to do justice, and to love kindness, and to walk humbly with your God?" Christians are not called to remain resentful. We are called to act in ways that are just. However, we are also commanded to forgive and, when possible, reconcile.

Resentment is a barrier to play because it binds us to the past rather than allowing us to live in the present. It is impossible to truly play if we are shackled to a painful experience. It is like trying to play a game of football while wearing a backpack loaded with two twenty-pound weights. We might be able to enjoy the game for a moment, but the burden will quickly suppress any joy. To truly play, we must confront the resentment. It has often been stated that a person is victimized twice when they do not forgive. They are the victim of the original offense, and they become victimized by the bitterness that ensues from not forgiving the person. I would say it makes us three times the victim since it deprives us of joy, and hence play, in the here and now.

Barrier 4: The Curse of the Clock

In his book *The Order of Time*, quantum physicist Carlo Rovelli discusses time and how it has been historically measured. Prior to the nineteenth century, time was measured locally around a sundial. The hours were marked by church bells. However, it was an imprecise science, in that bells rang at different times. Furthermore, depending on the town's position to the sun, midday was different in one town than in neighboring regions. In the nineteenth century, rail travel necessitated a uniform measurement of time. For trains to travel precisely from one town to the next, time had to be standardized to ensure delays did not occur—a measurement that transcended localized estimations.

Living by the dictates of time has only become more heightened. Today, with globalization and an interconnected world, time controls our lives as never before. It is not uncommon for a home to have fifteen to twenty clocks. Typically, each room in our houses has a clock, if not multiple ones. And this does not include our phones and watches. We are surrounded by reminders of time. The outcome of this reality is that we are always mentally evaluating whether we are ahead of schedule, on time, or behind schedule. We partition our day into segments based on time. In essence, time governs our lives rather than us governing time. As a result, we do not give ourselves permission to breathe. We are either chasing or fighting time. How often do you say to yourself, "I just don't have enough time"? Or you lament, "I have so much to do." It is true that life involves responsibilities and commitments. Yet living by the clock can suppress one's ability to play, by squeezing life. We become conditioned to think that there are too many tasks or to-dos to complete in a day, thus believing, "I simply do not have *time* to celebrate life today. Maybe tomorrow."

Barrier 5: Unbalanced Theology

I fully affirm the doctrine of total depravity that states humans are completely sinful. It is biblical. It diagnoses the problem with the human condition. It upholds the necessity of the crucifixion and resurrection. It is our sinfulness that required God's justice to be administered on the cross. As humans, we are broken and in need of a savior.

However, this focus on human sinfulness has been elevated above other equally important truths. As humans, we are made in the image of God. As such, we are endowed with unique beauty, competencies, and goodness. Our image is marred due to sin; however, it is not completely devoid of goodness. We display God's image when we act generously, reach out with kindness, and enjoy life fully. God desires for us to be image bearers, which includes embodying the goodness and beauty inherent in the godhead.

Once again, to be clear, we need to understand both truths. But the problem with an unbalanced focus on human depravity over and above being created in the image of God is that it defines our reality in purely negative terms. It frames us by our need for restoration and redemption, without any capacity for good. When our mental framework is bracketed by the negative, it leads to a fixation on spiritual development. We feel compelled to pursue improvement; we strive to overcome our moral failures. In other words, we suppress play by fixating on personal growth. We think we need to *become* rather than *be*.

Another outcome of an unbalanced focus on human depravity is adopting an attitude of judgment toward the world. When depravity becomes the sole theological foundation for life, the church's mission can easily become communicating that truth to the world or judging the world because of it. We look through the lens of what is wrong with the world. This perspective paints the world as only contaminated and cursed without acknowledging its beauty.

How different might our perspective be if we affirmed human depravity while at the same time declaring God's goodness? God's common grace constrains the full effects of sin in this world. This allows us to appreciate God's beauty through creation. Further, it enables humans to display flares of goodness—one to another. As humans made in the image of God, we have the capacity to celebrate God's beauty in this world both internally and in his creation. This balanced outlook allows us to wrestle with impacts of the Fall while at the same time playing in God's creation without crippling guilt and defeat.

Barrier 6: Backgrounds

We are influenced by our backgrounds. Your personal upbringing frames how you see reality. Psychologist Jean Piaget discovered play to be an important aspect of childhood development. It is how we understand and categorize reality. Interestingly and sadly, we outgrow play in our lives. Life becomes more structured and rigid. Perhaps this is one reason we have a hard time unraveling life's difficulties.

If you were raised in an abusive and oppressive home, it is quite possible that you are developmentally scarred. This trauma then shapes your future relationships and life perspectives. Individuals in authority are perhaps seen as unsafe. Or it is challenging to be transparent with another person due to wanting to shield yourself from potential pain. It can even impact your view of God, so that you find him to be stern and harsh rather than a loving father (Rom. 8:15).

Children raised in abusive homes do not experience the innocence of play. Play was not safe if it was present at all. One can imagine the impact such deforming realities have on long-term development, particularly as it relates to play. If a person during these formative periods of life is not permitted to play, play in the future can be viewed suspiciously or lead to guilt. Sentiments such as "If I play, I might be punished" shout in the back of the mind.

In other cases, it is your religious background that prevents you from enjoying play. Certain denominations have constructed elaborate rules and requirements that suffocate life. To belong to such traditions, you must strictly abide by certain behavioral and doctrinal standards. Oftentimes, these rules are presented with a spiritual swath to encourage allegiance. While Christian conduct is important, Jesus warned of the danger of fixating on rules (Matt. 23:13–15). Play is permissive; rules are restrictive. Thus, one can see the tension that exists when one's religious experience has been largely defined by what one cannot do. It cripples one's ability to enjoy life. It restricts permission to play.

Barrier 7: Division

This final barrier seems to be a more current reality in society and the church. Division is becoming a given in society rather than an occurrence. Society is becoming increasingly polarized. Politics have divided communities and homes; it has weaponized ideas and beliefs. And social media has become a forum to exploit this division.

Sadly, this division is not simply a societal reality; the church has become an extension of the fracturing. In some circles, the church has been the cause of the division. We are fully at odds with one another. People with different opinions from us are seen as antagonists; fellow Christians are deemed the enemy simply because of a different viewpoint.

Jesus prayed in John 17:22–23, "The glory that you have given me I have given to them, that they may be one even as we are one, I in them and you in me, that they may become perfectly one, so that the world may know that you sent me and loved them even as you loved me." He desires unity, not uniformity. Yet, increasingly so, there is a mandate for uniformity. If someone holds a different perspective, they are viewed as errant. Whether in society or in the church, it is becoming gradually more difficult to feel safe.

We know from childhood experiences that safety is necessary to play. If one does not feel safe on the playground, one cannot enjoy play. That person will feel guarded. For example, if a person is invited to participate in a game of pick-up basketball knowing that they will be mocked or scorned, even though they might participate in the game, they will be unable to embrace play. They will feel self-conscious. Similarly, if the church is no longer a safe place, it becomes nearly impossible to play in that arena. I recently heard a person say to me, "The church used to be safe. It was a place I could be. It is no longer the case. I do not feel safe in the very place where I should feel the safest." I doubt this person will feel permission to play, at least not among those individuals or in that setting.

If we as Christians are not able to play in the church, it does not bode well for us cultivating a lifestyle of play—one supported and affirmed by our fellow Christians.

SUMMARIZING THOUGHTS

In a non-sinful world, play would be natural, spontaneous, and normal. Unfortunately, we live in a sinful world. As a result, play becomes suppressed and suffocated. It is no longer natural or normal to play, particularly as adults. Play requires focus and attention. To embody play in our lives, it is necessary to face the barriers that challenge play and to address them head-on. Otherwise, play becomes an occasional moment rather than a life-giving reality in our lives. It is possible to overcome these barriers. Yet it requires a renewed focus to enjoy the present moment in front of us. The psalmist urges God's people to celebrate life, "This is the day that the LORD has made; let us rejoice and be glad in it" (Ps. 118:24).

REFLECTION

In 1991, I backpacked through Europe. It was an incredible experience seeing beautiful cities and amazing sights. One of my stops was in Rome to see a friend studying at the Vatican. Since I had never been to Rome, he treated me to a private tour of the Vatican. I anticipated the tour being amazing. However, I soon realized the purpose of the tour was not the sights but the experience. At each stop, he would provide the history of that statue or painting. He wanted me to appreciate each corner of St. Peter's Basilica. When we encountered a member of the Swiss Guard, we would stop and talk with that person. I would hear about the person's background and how he came to work at the Vatican. There were times we laughed. There were times we admired the beauty of the architecture. And there were times we were silent. We were not rushed. We were not looking at our watches. We simply settled in for the day. He wanted me to enjoy the experience of this moment—to be and to enjoy. Oh, this was very different than a professional tour guide, where as soon as you see one sight, you are quickly rushed to the next sight so that you get your money's worth.

I sincerely do not want the rest of this book to be a quick read. I hope you do not feel rushed. I pray it is transformative. I want it to be an experience. I want it to be enjoyed slowly, not quickly. I hope it is like that Vatican tour that allowed me to settle into it—processing it, absorbing it, living it. If you can do so, you just might begin to enjoy life—to play.

As we close out this chapter, spend some time pondering the following reflection questions. I want you to think about the barriers mentioned in this chapter. Which barriers resonate with you most? What are the obstacles that prevent you from playing? What is suffocating your ability to play?

1. Reflect on these past few years. How much did you play? I don't mean leisure activity, but rather: How much did you embody genuine playfulness?

2. What is the primary barrier preventing you from playing?

3. How has your upbringing shaped your view of play?

4. What attitude shifts do you believe will help you move toward playfulness?

5. Does your theology allow for play?

CHAPTER 3

Learning to Love Me: Playing in My Identity

You see a child play, and it is so close to seeing an artist paint, for in play a child says things without uttering a word. You can see how he solves his problems. You can also see what's wrong. Young children, especially, have enormous creativity, and whatever's in them rises to the surface in free play.

—Erik Erikson

This chapter is a challenge to love the person God has created you to be. It is not a promotion of narcissism. Immediately, you might be cautious, based on the title, "Learning to love me." I am not promoting radical individualism. I am not advocating egocentric love. I am not encouraging the elevation of self in a form of self-idolatry. Rather, I am suggesting that we need to love ourselves as God-created and God-formed beings if we are to play.

There are numerous things that prevent us from playing, one being dissatisfaction with self. If we don't enjoy who we are, it will pose a significant barrier to playing. Let us consider the childhood activity of play. For children to truly play, it is essential for them to enjoy one another. For example, there were occasions when my children were young and someone they did not like asked them to play. You could see it in their disengaged posture and disinterested voice. "OK, I have nothing else to do. I guess I will go play with them. But do I really have to?" They didn't even want to be around the person, let alone play. In this case, play became a chore rather than a delight. In contrast, when their best friend called to hang out, they looked for any reason to play, even turning off their favorite TV show. They could not wait to play. The reason is quite simple. They *liked* the one person and did not like the other. Critical to liberating and enjoyable play is liking the other person.

This is true for us. To play, we need to like ourselves. I must like me. If I don't like me, then I don't want to even be around me, and thus I will not play. I define play as *the God-given ability and permission to fully enjoy moments in life as God intended, with freedom and pleasure.* If I want to fully enjoy moments of play, I need to like the person who is always present in every moment of my life—me. Since play is not defined as an activity but a way of living, this truth becomes even more important. In this chapter, I want to explore the different aspects of our lives that we might not like. It might be your personality. It might be your appearance. It might be this season in your life. I hope that unpacking these aspects will move you toward loving the person God has created you to be.

WHY IDENTITY?

Identity is the core of who we are. It is the essence of who I am. It is the true me. It is how I think about myself, and it frames how I see life. Our identities are both created by God, as his beautiful creations, and nurtured throughout life. God fashioned us uniquely with specific characteristics. They are innate to us, such as appearance and personality. Yet our identity is also shaped by the experiences and relationships, historic and present, in our lives. It is always developing.

Erik Erikson pioneered research on identity development. He believed development occurred through eight stages, from infancy to adulthood, with the adolescent stage characterizing a struggle between identity and role confusion as a person wrestles over self-conception within social contexts. A person avoids role confusion when they begin to discover their personal philosophy of life (1968, 598–610). James Marcia expanded Erikson's theory, developing four identity statuses that combine exploration of identity and commitment to that identity (Berk 2008, 316). The healthiest statuses are *identity achievement*, describing individuals who are committed to a set of values and beliefs, and *identity moratorium*, encompassing persons who are wrestling with their identity. Considered unhealthy, *identity foreclosure* explains individuals who accept values and beliefs without assessing them, while *identity diffusion* characterizes persons that do not commit to values or beliefs (Patterson, Sochting, and Marcia 1992, 9–24). For many, it is not uncommon to wrestle with one's identity. And struggles with identity are not isolated to adolescence; they occur throughout one's life. A teenager goes off to college, where she questions her Christian roots and thus reevaluates whether God's affirmations of her are true. At the same time, a parent might now face an empty nest, thus having to reorient his identity around separation from the child. Relationally, a newlywed's identity is redefined by the oneness that occurs through marriage. Or, later in life, individuals facing retirement oftentimes encounter identity moratorium, as they are no longer defined by their vocation and thus wonder, Who am I now?

Many individuals journey through life struggling toward identity achievement. Their identity is being framed by friends, society, or work, thus causing them to experience identity foreclosure or diffusion. As a result, they do not know or embrace their unique identity but rather adhere to an identity shaped by others or shifting based on circumstances. In other cases, individuals are committed to an identity; however, it is one that is not aligned to a biblical worldview. It is common today to embrace individualism, which views persons as free agents determining their own identity—"I am who I choose to be." Or sin is accepted as part of one's identity ("I was born this way") rather than seeing sin as marring one's identity.

The remedy is to allow our identities to be principally framed by God, particularly in the midst of shifting seasons in our lives. Our identities will be stretched and reoriented. It is natural. It is normal. However, to avoid unhealthy identity formation, we must anchor our view of self in God and his view of us. St. Augustine of Hippo is credited as saying, "God loves each one of us as if there were only one of us to love" (Dunning 1988, 197). God loves us passionately. He loves us unconditionally. He loves us perfectly. God sees us as his beloved sons or daughters, worthy of his affection.

Embracing God's view of us allows us to ground our identity in his transcendent affirmations and promises. Shifting will still occur, but it will be anchored in a God-identity. To use a visual, an oak tree sways and is even damaged during a storm. However, because it is rooted, it stays grounded and firm, thus allowing it to be stabilized and even regenerate lost limbs after the storm. Its essence as an oak tree does not change even though its form may be altered because of the winds. Similarly, our identities will sway due to seasons in life (moving away from home, marriage, retirement) or difficulties (passing of a loved one, cancer diagnosis, abuse). But if we can center our view of self in a God-identity, it allows us to stay grounded regardless of life's storms. In other words, identity achievement for the Christian occurs when our view of self aligns with God's view of us—"I am who he says I am."

HOW DOES IDENTITY CONNECT TO PLAY?

You might be thinking, "I thought we were supposed to be talking about play. We seem to have taken a detour into identity." For me, this detour is critically important to achieving play in our lives. Imagine you are a baseball or softball player. You thoroughly love the game. It is not difficult for you to practice because the sport energizes you. It is easy to spend hours throwing the ball. Over the course of time, you find yourself becoming an excellent pitcher. The ball is pinpoint accurate as it crosses the plate. It does so with the right amount of movement and speed. The only caveat is that your form is unorthodox. Rather than throwing in a conventional way, you have discovered your arm throws best when it is released from the side rather than overhand or underhand. When you try out for the team, the coaches are fascinated with your potential. Yet they believe you would be most successful if your form was fixed to conform to an orthodox approach. The assistant coaches go to work. They begin to instruct you. They send you to clinics where experts film your arm movement and recommend you altering everything from your stance to your hand placement on the ball.

You love the game; therefore, you listen attentively to every piece of advice, striving to implement their recommendations. You desperately desire to be the pitcher *they want you to be*. With every slight adjustment, you notice your love for the game plummeting. You are no longer playing the game; you are chasing someone else's ideal for how you should play the game. Every time you throw the ball, you hear a myriad of voices whispering, "Throw it like this. Hold the ball firmly in this position." You find yourself hating the game rather than loving it. Playing the game has become a chore.

Contrast this scenario with one where a coach sees your unique form and decides to harness it, not change it. He sees the potential in you within your specific skills and throwing motion. He provides some tweaks and instructions but does not dramatically alter your approach to throwing the ball. He affirms your unique approach to pitching. And he encourages you to enjoy the game. Likely, you would find your love for the game soaring and your unique gifts blossoming. Playing the game in this scenario is quite natural and life-giving.

This is an analogy of our identity. We oftentimes chase identities. Someone makes a negative comment about our performance, so we alter it to measure up to their standard. A supervisor declares that a successful person should act like this; therefore, we conform our behavior to fit this mold. An advertisement paints a specific picture of beauty. Quickly, we overhaul our appearance to be "attractive." Over time, we find these whispers in our head pulling us in different directions toward someone else's ideal. The more we chase, the more life becomes a chore—"I will never measure up." It is hard to *enjoy moments in life, with freedom and pleasure*, when you feel inadequate in the eyes of others. Those voices become the dominant ones, and they are rarely life-giving.

God uniquely created us and knows us. He does not desire to overhaul our unique make-up because he is the one who made it. He wants to harness it for his purposes. He wants our God-identity to be true to us, not molded in the ideals of someone else. He desires to be the sole voice in our minds, shaping and guiding us. As the giver of life, God alone can be the voice that is most life-giving. When we can rest in this identity, it allows us to be present in life, in the moment, with the capacity to play. Playing is *most natural within our God-given and God-shaped identity*. It is the place that is most free. It is the place that is safest. And it is the place with the most pleasure.

HOW GOD SEES ME

In the next few pages, I would like to unpack our God-identity, beginning with how God sees us. Genesis 1:27 frames our true identity: "So God

created man in his own image, in the image of God he created him; male
and female he created them." We are made in God's image. At our core,
we are reflections of God. God's fingerprints are imprinted on us. This is
true regardless of our faith. Our acceptance of Christ does not determine
our status as image bearers of God. It is true of every human, Christian
and non-Christian. This reality should produce great esteem in us. We are
fashioned after the Creator of the universe. Theologians sometimes emphasize God's transcendence or intimacy, struggling to find a balance between
the two. These two realities find a meeting place in our nature, as we are
fashioned by a transcendent God yet in a unique and intimate manner.

These two truths are expressed in Psalm 139:13–16:

> For you formed my inward parts;
>   you knitted me together in my mother's womb.
> I praise you, for I am fearfully and wonderfully made.
> Wonderful are your works;
>   my soul knows it very well.
> My frame was not hidden from you,
> when I was being made in secret,
>   intricately woven in the depths of the earth.
> Your eyes saw my unformed substance;
> in your book were written, every one of them,
>   the days that were formed for me,
>   when as yet there was none of them.

I love this passage because it captures the intentional intimacy of God.
Reflect on the language in these verses. As you do, imagine a focused and
perfectionist knitter or inventor. Someone who meticulously attends to
his task with great care and precision. A perfectionist is not satisfied with
sloppy work. This is God.

He "formed" and "knitted" *our physical being* exactly to his perfect
imagination. In addition, he made us "fearfully and wonderfully." *Our
personality and our interests* are fashioned with a careful attention to
detail. God "intricately" created us. There is no flaw to his work, for such
a flaw would reflect that he is flawed. Since he is perfect, he makes us

perfectly. This passage extends beyond our being to our life experiences and relationships—"in your book were written, every one of them, the days that were formed for me." Our identities are crafted and supervised by a loving God. We are beautiful and perfect in the eyes of the Creator. Later in this chapter we will discuss how sin has marred us, yet it does not nullify our beauty as God's creations.

When an artist produces a masterpiece, he does not look at it and degrade it. He delights in it. When an inventor creates something that is life-changing, she does not hide it. Rather, she showcases it. This is God's view of us. We are masterpieces to him. Every new parent looks for opportunities to display pictures of their newborn child. In every aspect, they are perfect. I imagine this is how God sees us, affectionately showcasing us to the heavenly host. If only we could fully embrace God's pride of us, it would radically change our self-perception.

What does it say, then, when we do not like ourselves? What are we saying about God as our creator? There were moments when our children would say something negative about themselves. They might say, "I am not very pretty." Or "I am not very smart." These were sentiments that emerged usually because of something that happened with classmates. In each instance, my wife would quickly state, "I don't want you to ever say that about yourself. You are intelligent. You are amazing. And you are beautiful. No child of mine will degrade themselves." The point she was pressing home is to not disparage oneself. Love who you are! This is how God wants us to see ourselves. I can imagine God saying, "No child of mine should degrade themselves!"

LOVING MYSELF

Jesus stated, "You shall love the Lord your God with all your heart and with all your soul and with all your mind. This is the great and first commandment. And a second is like it: You shall love your neighbor as yourself" (Matt. 22:37–39). We are to love God. We are to love our neighbor. And we are to love ourselves. How do we love ourselves? I would like to provide two practical areas that powerfully influence our identity: appearance and personality. I selected these two areas because they are common struggles for most people.

Love Your Appearance

Athletic. Thin. Attractive. Young.

These are qualities that are esteemed in our society. We live in a media world where the beautiful are idolized; all others receive second place. Despite the recent trends to promote body image, the undercurrent in society remains—it is better to be modelesque. The natural result in such a society is to despise ourselves. We look in the mirror and quickly find faults in our appearance. We dread shopping because we presume there is nothing that will look good on us. Our minds are fixated on the person who seems "prettier" or "more built" than us.

This fixation has an intrusive impact on our ability to play. Playing involves being in the moment—seeing God's goodness in life. It seeks to celebrate that we are made beautiful by the Creator. It is impossible to play if we are constantly comparing ourselves to others. When we engage in self-talk that says, "I am inferior to everyone else," it sabotages our ability to be.

When our kids were young, they played soccer. We would go to the games excited to cheer our children on. They were just starting out, so we were not concerned about their performance as much as enjoying the game. One season, our daughter had a coach that loved to critique. Throughout the entire game, he would bark out instructions. He would call children over in the middle of the game and tell them what they were doing wrong. At times, he would even come out on the field and move a child to a different position. This criticism had a significant impact on their ability to enjoy the game. They became anxious. They stopped running. At times, they became paralyzed, uncertain what to do. They stopped *playing* because they were so concerned of doing something wrong. Living in society oftentimes paralyzes us. We are so concerned about measuring up to others that we stop living. Because we feel inferior to a societal standard, we stop living in the moment. We stop enjoying ourselves. We stop playing.

God wants us to play in our identity. This includes celebrating the truth that we are physical masterpieces regardless of whether we have a disability, unattractive quality, or physical limitation. In the eyes of God, we are masterpieces. By distancing ourselves from cultural or self-inflicted messages that diminish our worth, we can freely enjoy ourselves. There are moments when we look in the mirror and feel great about our appearance. You know those days. Your hair looks good. The outfit looks perfect. You smile as you do a final check. In that moment, your disposition is lifted. You feel confident. You feel happy. You are ready to enjoy the day. The positive view of yourself enables you to be playful. This mindset should be the norm rather than the exception because we are knit by the Master Knitter.

Love Your Personality

We live in a world that promotes the charismatic, extroverted person. This is the individual who is the life of the party. Susan Cain, in her book on introverts titled *Quiet*, highlighted the messages that bombard us and extol us to be outgoing. These messages ranged from Nike's slogan "Just do it" to Amtrak's "Depart from your inhibitions." These ads cultivate a belief that outgoing people have more fun. They are more liked. They will have better opportunities in life. And we buy into it. Research has indicated that extroverted personalities experience greater vocational possibilities. Leadership positions are oftentimes given to extroverts more than introverts, not because of proven ability to lead but due to the presumption that extroverts are better leaders. The reason for this sentiment is the belief that outgoing people make the best leaders. Charisma is king in our culture. Certainly relational competency is an essential skill to being a good leader but it is not the only thing. A charismatic individual can equally be a poor leader.

Further, Cain discussed the evangelical fixation on extroversion. She described how the typical evangelical church caters to extroverts—the "stand up and greet the person around you," the small group discussions, and the testimonials. For me, I cringe when I visit a church and they ask people to greet the person around you. As an introvert, I just want to be present. We visited a church in Chicago once where the pastor asked all first-time visitors to stand. My kids immediately looked at my wife and me as if to say, "What? They are going to make us stand in front of strangers? If they bring a microphone over to me, I am out of here." To be fair, I have no problem with hospitality. We should welcome people. It is also good for the church to spotlight how God is working in the lives of other people. Testimonies powerfully communicate biblical truths. And small groups are intimate forums to dig into the Scriptures. Yet these trappings can also cultivate, as Cain stated, a "Culture of Personality" (Cain 2013, 21, referencing Susman 2003, 271–85). It elevates a specific personality type as more spiritual, more Christian.

There is a tendency to not like one's personality. I wish I was more like the popular person. I wish I was more of a leader. I wish I was more outgoing. It can also cut the other way. I wish I could sit still. I wish I could be content just being by myself. I wish I could be happy simply enjoying a book. It is normal to want to change certain things about ourselves. Yet, it is important to remember that it is incredibly hard to change one's personality. In fact, we could very well be fighting a losing battle. Research indicates that personality is largely framed from birth. While environment does play a role in the construction of one's personality, genetic studies indicate that up to 60 percent of one's personality type is determined by genetics (Sanchez-Roige 2018). If this is true, most of our temperament is largely set before we take a breath.

God fearfully and wonderfully made us. This includes our personality. And yet we fight against our nature. We strive to be someone we are not simply because we believe it would be better to have a different temperament. In doing so, we are rejecting God's unique knitting of us. I enjoyed the '90s TV show *Home Improvement*. It starred Tim Allen as Tim Taylor, a host of the show *Tool Time*, which focused on demonstrating and testing tools. Throughout the program, Tim enjoyed souping up tools. He would tinker with a nail gun to get more power. He took apart his leaf blower and rebuilt the motor so it had the force of a jet engine. Not surprisingly, each experiment ended poorly. To the viewer, it was common sense. The leaf blower was never designed to house a jet engine. The inventor had a unique design and purpose for that product. Altering it changed the product and damaged it. It would not work properly if altered.

God created us with a unique personality. We work best when we live within that personality. It aligns with God's purpose for us. Striving to change that personality is not only futile (we are genetically made this way) but tragically says, "God, the way you made me is not good enough." Honestly, that is audacious to say to the perfect Creator.

How does this connect to play? If we are busy striving to change ourselves into a perceived better version, we will not enjoy the very temperament God gave to us. To use a childhood example, children who are uncomfortable with their personality have difficulty fitting in. Imagine the scene where an introverted child is reluctant to participate in a game with a group of extroverts. The extroverts are giving high fives. They are celebrating with gusto after every score. There is a lot of energy. The introvert attempts to be exuberant. He tries to smile and holler with excitement. However, it is forced. He is trying to be an extrovert even though he is not. As a result, he is unable to be fully in the moment. The same would be the case for an extrovert being asked to fit into an introverted context.

This is true of us adults. At times, we are so preoccupied with image (being someone we are not) in the hopes of being liked that play becomes a task rather than an opportunity to enjoy others. Striving to change our personality can be exhausting. We should embrace our personality. We should enjoy our personality. We should rest in our personality. When we can accept and like our personality, we will be able to play because we are content with who we are. It frees us from the distraction of pursuing a different "me" so that we can be at home in the unique "me."

WHERE DOES DISLIKE OF SELF COME FROM?

The disconnect between how God sees us and how we see ourselves is a result of sin in the world. Sin has marred our image. It has not destroyed our image; it has corrupted it. A colleague described it as "sin vandalizing our image." I like this! The original image is still present, like a vandalized painting or wall; it just has been marred. The good news is it can be restored!

Romans 5:12 states, "Sin came into the world through one man, and death through sin, and so death spread to all men because all sinned." Sin entered the world through Adam, from whom it entered every person. This sin mars our image. Paul wrote in 1 Corinthians 15:48–49, "As was the man of dust, so also are those who are of the dust, and as is the man of heaven, so also are those who are of heaven. Just as we have borne the image of the man of dust, we shall also bear the image of the man of heaven." These verses describe the tension between God's original design for us as made in the image of God and the impact of sin on that image. Some theologians have espoused the belief that the image of God in us is destroyed due to sin. I do not find this biblically accurate, since the image of God is mentioned in numerous passages post-Fall (Gen. 5:1, 3; 9:6). Nor does this view coincide with reality. Non-Christians can display incredible acts of goodness. They can be generous. They can be sacrificial. They can be good spouses and excellent parents. These qualities could not occur if the image of God in them was destroyed; only sin would dominate.

We therefore live in this tension between being made perfect in God's image and the marring of that image by sin. To resolve this tension, it is important to affirm several important truths. First, we must discern between what is good, embedded in our divine nature, and what is sinful, a distorted expression. We should celebrate that which is good—our personality, our physical appearance, and our interests. Yet we should suppress, tame, and confess those expressions that are not good—a personality that is controlling, vanity, and immoral interests. That which God has made beautiful, sin strives to mar. It is the vandalizer!

Second, it is commonplace in the church to throw the baby out with the bathwater. We emphasize sin so much—its distorting and oppressive nature—that we forget, if not dismiss, the beautiful reality that we are still made in the image of God. Even though we are broken, our base nature is beautiful. We need to celebrate this truth. Realistically distinguishing and separating out God's view of us as "fearfully and wonderfully made" from our broken nature enables us to play. It opens the door to love ourselves—*not the sinful me but the made-in-the-image-of-God me*. It allows us to play within our identity, the one God intimately fashioned and nurtures.

THE PLAYGROUND TERRORIST

Satan is the quintessential playground terrorist who prevents us from enjoying moments in life. He uses sin to degrade and mock us. He enjoys agitating sentiments of inferiority and insecurity. He wants us to feel ridiculed. He desires for us to be so fixated on hating ourselves that we are unable to enjoy a playful moment. Satan strives to destroy us (1 Peter 5:8). He is a liar (John 8:44). He seeks to amplify our sin nature to the point where we become defined by our sin rather than God. One of his tactics is to debase our identity. At times, he directly assaults us by whispering in our ears with demeaning thoughts, such as "Everyone thinks you are a nobody." Other times, he is indirect, using other people, circumstances, or societal messages to strip us of worth.

Jesus stated, "The thief comes only to steal and kill and destroy. I came that they may have life and have it abundantly" (John 10:10). A chief strategy of the thief is to attack our identity—to beat us down like a playground bully. For many, this attack on their identity has had lifelong consequences. You strive to shake the powerful voice that strips and guts you of your God-given identity. In contrast, Jesus affirms the abundant life. He desires that we understand and embrace our true worth in God. In the next verse, Jesus referenced his eventual sacrifice: "The good shepherd lays down his life for the sheep" (v. 11). Christ died so that we could have the abundant life—a life freed from the taunts of Satan, the playground bully. The cross enables us to enjoy a redeemed identity in Christ.

In verse 14 of this passage, Jesus stated, "I am the good shepherd. I know my own and my own know me." Christians are known by the Good Shepherd, not only as image bearers of God but as those redeemed through the cross. God knows and nurtures our true selves, our true identities. And, through the cross, we have the capacity to intimately know the one who affirms and elevates these identities.

GOD DESIRES OUR IDENTITIES TO FLOURISH

Identity formation is a natural part of life. God built identity development into humanity and deemed it to be a normal and natural process. It is not an automatic process; it occurs over the course of one's life. And because our identities are influenced by sin, identity development involves surrendering to God's formative process. Isaiah 64:8 states, "But now, O Lord, you are our Father; we are the clay, and you are our potter; we are all the work of your hand." God molds us throughout our lives, and this molding process includes our identities. This process is designed to build trust in God. He desires that we discern the formative processes and shaping in our lives as we experience life moments and life transitions. When we see God working to transform our identities in a way that nurtures a God-identity, we should affirm and embrace it. In contrast, when our identities are pulled in a way that is humanistic and egocentric, we need to dismiss and turn from those influences. As a result, there is the necessity to wrestle with our identities, referred to above as identity moratorium. It is God's way of deepening our relationships with him, moving us toward achieving God-identities.

Play involves discovery. Returning to the baseball or softball example, learning these sports necessitates identifying one's strengths and weaknesses. To be successful in the transformation from a novice to a proficient player requires listening attentively to that coach who desires to harness one's unique giftedness. It involves *discovering* who one is and the type of player one can be. Playing in one's identity entails discovering what God is doing in us through life's development process and during life's transitions. We can play within our identities by participating in God's formative processes in our lives, even if they are at times difficult, knowing that his ultimate goal is to mold us into his beautiful image.

THE TOUGH TIMES

Transformative learning states that we learn most powerfully when we engage in self-examination following a disorienting event (Eschenbacher and Fleming 2020). In other words, discomfort rattles our stagnancy, thus allowing us to change. Scripture clearly states that God utilizes pain for his transformative purposes (Rom. 5:3–4). As C. S. Lewis said in *The Problem of Pain*, "God whispers to us in our pleasures, speaks in our conscience, but shouts in our pain; it is His megaphone to rouse a deaf world" (Lewis 2001, 91). As such, traumatic life moments, stretching experiences, and painful realities are used by God to shape our identities. The moments when we struggle with identity, such as leaving for college or entering retirement, are seasons used by God to mold us into his image. We often resist these moments because they are uncomfortable. In these situations, we should instead discern what God is doing in our lives and how he is shaping us. This process involves *discovery*, not escape.

It is possible that you are not able to see how or in what way you are being molded. You might find yourself depressed and frustrated, asking yourself, "What is God doing? I understand he is developing me, but I have no clue as to what he is doing. I wish he would just show me." Or you might be wondering, "Where is God? He seems to have forgotten about me." These sentiments can easily make you feel stuck or hopeless.

Because you are paralyzed, you are not able to play. You find moments of pleasure impossible because of the struggle to know your identity in the moment. When you see others playing, you might envy them because they seem to know who they are and where they are heading. Understanding one's identity (and how God is forming it) most certainly impacts our ability to enjoy moments in life.

There are no easy answers. We never fully know what God is doing or how he is doing it. It is only by looking backward that we see his fingerprints. It is possible you might never know this side of heaven. The reality of the unknown can be frustrating. Yet Scripture is clear about these two truths: God is good, and he is molding you. In the tough times, it is important to rest, even uncomfortably, in these truths. Even if resting in God's work is tortuous (and it likely will be at times), it truly is the safest place to be.

Psalm 46 describes the turbulent nature of life—"the earth gives way" (v. 2) and "the nations rage" (v. 6). Yet in the midst of this chaos, we are encouraged to "Be still, and know that [God is] God" (v. 10). Perhaps stillness is necessary for you so that you can unravel the disorienting moments in your life. It is possible that play has been squelched because you are desperate to find direction and purpose. You are striving to find identity achievement, yet it is elusive. Resting in God's secure hands, even when facing the unknown, could open you up to the possibility of enjoying moments in life. Play can become possible when you trust God's molding even when you do not understand the what or the why. It is dancing in the rain after a horrific workday. It is the spontaneous game in the back yard following an unsettling health report. It is the belly laugh after you experience a conflict with a friend. Certainly, difficult times will likely require venting and even mourning. They might involve spending time in prayer or a long walk to process the events. Yet play is possible even in the tough times as long as we remain focused on the one who loves us and is molding us. In chapter 10, we will explore more deeply how to play when life is excruciatingly painful. It is hard, but it is possible.

SUMMARIZING THOUGHTS

Our identity is shaped by numerous factors—physical appearance, innate personality, relational connections, vocational status, and so on.

However, ultimately, our identity is defined by God. As the Creator, he is intimately and carefully knitting us into his beautiful, beloved creation. We are his children. And nothing the world communicates to us changes this truth. When we fully embrace this true reality as dearly loved children, we have the capacity to enjoy life fully—to play—because we are rooted in the correct perspective of ourselves: God's! And when we see life's difficulties and transitions as God's arena to mold us, we are able to play within our identities even in those circumstances by discovering his intimate purposes for us.

REFLECTION

As we close out this chapter, think about how you view yourself. God intimately and beautifully created you. Do you love who God is forming you to be? Do you trust that God is molding you beautifully into his image?

1. Reflect on your dissatisfactions. What are you most dissatisfied about? Why are you feeling this way? What does this dissatisfaction say about your view of God?

2. What messages of the world are you currently buying into that cause personal dissatisfaction?

3. What things would you change about yourself? Reflect on these thoughts and spend time in Scripture asking God to give you an accurate picture of yourself. How does God see you?

4. Look in the mirror. Take a few moments and remind yourself that you are beautifully and intimately made by the *Master Knitter*. Perhaps post Psalm 139:13–16 on your bathroom mirror to remind yourself that God loves you, his creation and his child.

5. Commit to playing in all circumstances of life, even the difficult moments, because as a dearly loved child of God, you can.

CHAPTER 4

Learning to Be: Playing in the Moment

> *You made us for yourself and our heart is restless until it rests in you.*
>
> —Augustine

This chapter is hard for me. I am a restless person. It is highly unusual for me to sit still for long periods of time. I take great pride in being efficient; therefore, it seems unproductive to simply be. Or more so, I *believe* it is unproductive to simply be. For me, there is joy in squeezing out of life every bit of margin so I feel accomplished at the end of the day. And by accomplished, I mean in my completion of tasks. Individuals who enjoy creating a list and checking off the items on that list fully understand me.

This chapter is thus hard for me because I feel ill-equipped to write on the importance of *being*. Playing in the moment is a foreign concept to me. Yet it is in confronting one's weakness that a person can grow. Therefore, I am approaching this chapter as part self-reflection and part personal longing. It is reflection in that the concepts in this chapter are a result of my own restlessness, namely, why it is difficult to be. It is longing in that it provides for me a hope that I will grow in my ability to be.

Playing in the moment would be medicinal for my life. It would allow me space to breathe. It would stir in me deep contentment, free from the shackles of always doing. In preparing for this chapter, I have wondered how much joy I have missed out on because of my compulsion to always be active. Restlessness suffocates one's ability to play.

SUCCESS

A deeply fond memory for me was a father-son trip to northern Pennsylvania. Since he was a child, my son Ryan has enjoyed the night sky. His fascination with the cosmos inspired me to love it as well. I remember numerous evenings watching the stars or planets with him, especially when constellation events were occurring. We would venture into our back yard, pull out his telescope, and gaze at the moon or Mars. I marvel at his amazement as the edges of a planet come into focus. For my son, looking at the night sky is a worshipful experience. He is drawn closer to God through creation.

For my birthday present one year, he gave me a trip to a dark sky park, a place shielded from city and artificial lights. They are set up around the country for stargazers—so people can truly see the fullness of the night sky with all its detail and clarity. Thankfully, there is one located a few hours from our house. Cherry Springs State Park is considered to have some of the darkest night skies on the East Coast of the United States. It is located at an altitude of twenty-three hundred feet and far away from any cities.

I remember the trip vividly because it began after a long week of teaching six eight-hour days. I was tired. As an introvert, I was a bit shredded from the student engagement. There was a side of me that wanted to grab my computer and fall asleep while watching a movie. Instead, I made an extra-strong cup of coffee, ran home, changed clothes, and hopped in the car with my son to get to the park before the sun set.

We arrived just as the sun was disappearing on the horizon. We quickly drove into the park, only to discover that people who go to dark sky parks are quite fanatical. Immediately, we were informed to turn off our headlights. Later, as we put up our tent for the evening, an angry man approached us, threatening to contact the ranger if we did not turn off our flashlight. Needless to say, the evening did not begin with me *being in the moment.*

However, something happened once we settled into our lawn chairs with five layers of clothes and two blankets wrapped around each of us.

(Did I mention that it was going to be a low of 35 degrees that night?) I remember leaning back and looking up at the stars. I could see the Milky Way stretching across the sky. It was breathtaking. It was awe-inspiring. It was worshipful. It caused a stillness to come over me.

For the next six hours, we looked up at the stars, talking about different planets and the shape of the constellations. We pulled out his telescope a few times to look at a distant unknown object. Time slipped away. We chatted. We had rich conversations. We laughed, mostly at the fanatics. And we played! I was in the moment—restful, relaxed, and enjoying life richly and deeply with my son. For me, it was a time I would cherish, not simply for the memory, but also as a reminder of the incredible life-giving nature of playing in the moment. For an evening, I had success at *being*.

Even today, I look back at that moment and wonder how rich my life would be if that were not an isolated event but a regular experience. How much lighter would my soul be if I were able to be in the moment more frequently? How much more natural and secure would my relationships be if I could play in the moment without planning or effort? How much fuller would my life be if I stopped obsessing over what I needed to do and regularly embraced spontaneous play?

WHY DO WE FIND IT DIFFICULT TO BE?

Before treatment, it is always wise to undergo diagnosis. Otherwise, we will inevitably try out different remedies in the hopes one might work, but with limited success. It is much wiser to truly understand the problem before employing a solution. Playing in the moment should be heart-driven, not another activity prompted by a busy life.

Why is it that we find it difficult to be? Before we look at the underlying condition, I would like to articulate the symptoms, particularly for those living in the Western world. The problem is we are fixated on either the past or the future. They consume our mind, preventing us from living in the moment.

We Are Obsessed with the Future

Life can be very intense. It involves numerous demands and responsibilities. For most of one's life, it consists of preparing for the future. As soon as you enter high school, you need to be thinking about college. Once you enter college, you need to position yourself for a career. After you get married, you begin to think about a family. Once your children leave the home, you prepare for your retirement. It seems that the only time a person is not thinking about the future is when they are a child. It is no wonder then that children have an easier time playing. They understand that they are a child with limited responsibilities; therefore, it is OK to play. Some children experience broken homes, or worse yet, do not even have homes, and thus face daily concerns and worries. However, for those raised in stable homes, children can be in the moment without immediate concerns for finances, protection, or stability.

Thinking about the future is not a bad thing. Jesus stated, "For which of you, desiring to build a tower, does not first sit down and count the cost, whether he has enough to complete it?" (Luke 14:28). Planning is not wrong; the problem lies in obsessing about the future. It is not uncommon for people to *always* be thinking about tomorrow. We plan for the weekend. We plan to get into college. We plan for the next day's work tasks. We plan for retirement. Even though we are physically present in the moment today, we might as well be living in the future, as our minds are fixated on tomorrow. We are obsessed with the future.

It is noteworthy that most references to planning in the Bible are embedded in the reality that God is sovereign over the future. Jeremiah 29:11 states, "For *I know the plans I have for you,* declares the LORD, plans for welfare and not for evil, to give you a future and a hope" (emphasis added). Proverbs 16:9 affirms, "The heart of man plans his way, *but the* LORD establishes his steps" (emphasis added). Planning is good *within the embrace of God's knowledge and authority over the future.* When we plan within this mindset, it is good because we are affirming God's direction and purposes. Yet it is more likely that our obsession with the future involves our desire to manage tomorrow rather than trust God for it.

This obsession typically results in worrying about the future. We are anxious about health concerns. We are nervous about job security and financial stability. We are worried about our relationships, or whether we will find a relationship. The worry is a response to the unknown. Uncertainty about the future makes us nervous at best and paralyzed at worst.

Jesus exhorted us to trust God for the future:

> Therefore I tell you, do not be anxious about your life, what
> you will eat or what you will drink, nor about your body, what
> you will put on. Is not life more than food, and the body more
> than clothing? Look at the birds of the air: they neither sow
> nor reap nor gather into barns, and yet your heavenly Father
> feeds them. Are you not of more value than they? And which
> of you by being anxious can add a single hour to his span of
> life? And why are you anxious about clothing? Consider the
> lilies of the field, how they grow: they neither toil nor spin, yet
> I tell you, even Solomon in all his glory was not arrayed like
> one of these. But if God so clothes the grass of the field, which
> today is alive and tomorrow is thrown into the oven, will he
> not much more clothe you, O you of little faith? Therefore do
> not be anxious, saying, "What shall we eat?" or "What shall
> we drink?" or "What shall we wear?" For the Gentiles seek
> after all these things, and your heavenly Father knows that
> you need them all. But seek first the kingdom of God and his
> righteousness, and all these things will be added to you.
>
> Therefore do not be anxious about tomorrow, for tomorrow
> will be anxious for itself. Sufficient for the day is its own trou-
> ble. (Matt. 6:25–34)

We should trust God for the future—for his provision and his care.
Someone encouraged me early on in life that "it is wise not to borrow
trouble from tomorrow." In essence, this person was challenging me to
not fret over things that I could not control—tomorrow's worries. Rather,
embrace today and trust God for tomorrow.

Playing involves being present in the moment. It is not possible to truly
play if we are thinking about tomorrow. Imagine a person playing a game of
volleyball with some friends. If the person was slightly crouched, with hands
prepped to set the ball, but thinking about tomorrow's business meeting, it
would be impossible for them to play. In fact, they might be so distracted

that they get hit with the ball. To effectively play—just from a physical standpoint, let alone emotionally—involves being present in the moment.

Is it possible to avoid planning for tomorrow? No. In fact, those who live entirely in the moment are likely irresponsible in many aspects of life. Thus, it is necessary to plan. We must think about our family's future needs. Chores and responsibilities require our attention. Vacations don't simply happen. As much as we might want to be laissez-faire and spontaneous, it is neither possible nor appropriate. Neither is it possible to never be anxious about tomorrow. It is a human response. Jesus's words prompt us to remember God's sovereignty and to trust in him, rather than feeling guilty from anxiety. It is human to worry about a health concern. It is appropriate to be concerned about the financial markets. It is loving to worry about our children's social acceptance and emotional health. The challenge is to bring these moments to God when they occur rather than trusting in our own human strength. If we can do so, we provide space in our lives for play.

We Are Reliving the Past

I compartmentalize life. At the end of a workday, I strive to close the necessary boxes so that I can be fully present at home. At times, I am successful. Other times, it is impossible. If I experience an incredibly frustrating day, the boxes spill over into my homelife. Other times, I am thinking about regrets from the previous day, wishing I had stated something differently or reacted in a more positive manner. You might have these moments as well, where you wish you could redo a previous day in the hopes of achieving a different outcome.

These are natural tendencies. Life is never perfect; therefore, we have regular regrets about life. Or we have too much work to contain it into a single day. As a result, we find it difficult to box tasks in. In some seasons of life or work, it can be quite frustrating because you feel like you are playing Whac-A-Mole simply to stay afloat. This inability to set aside yesterday's concerns prevents us from playing in the present.

There have been numerous occasions when I was listening to my wife's day, only to be mentally closing filing drawers in my head. Worse yet, there have been times when my family began vacation, only for me to still be mentally working. We were seeing beautiful sights; however, I was not enjoying them, since I was still processing work tasks. When my wife and I were serving as pastor and wife, it was not uncommon for us to process ministry on the first day of vacation. We would be traveling to our destination and unpacking congregational concerns or decisions. The vacation had physically begun, but mentally we were still working. Rather than stepping into moments of play, our preoccupation with the past held us captive.

God stated in Isaiah, "Remember not the former things, nor consider the things of old. Behold, I am doing a new thing; now it springs forth, do you not perceive it?" (43:18–19). In order to see what God is doing in the present, it is essential to stop dwelling on the past. Living in the past prevents us from enjoying God's "new things" today.

You might be thinking that I have minimized deep pain in a person's life. For the purposes of this chapter, I am thinking of everyday busyness—relationally or vocationally. In chapter 7, I will address more fully how to handle the wounds we have experienced in life.

The Real Problem: Control

Reliving the past and obsessing over the future are symptoms of a deeper problem—our desire for control. At the heart of our fixation over past regrets and the unknown future is a hope that somehow we can control life events. This is birthed in a humanistic mindset focused on self that erroneously inflates our importance and illusion of control. When cultivated, we begin to assume we have the ability to manipulate life's outcomes. Further, this mindset erodes a God-centered worldview—one that affirms God's transcendence over time—past, present, and future. Isaiah 46 states,

> Remember this and stand firm,
>   recall it to mind, you transgressors,
>   remember the former things of old;
> for I am God, and there is no other;
>   I am God, and there is none like me,
> declaring the end from the beginning
>   and from ancient times things not yet done,

saying, "My counsel shall stand,
    and I will accomplish all my purpose,"
calling a bird of prey from the east,
    the man of my counsel from a far country.
I have spoken, and I will bring it to pass;
    I have purposed, and I will do it. (vv. 8–11)

A biblical theology declares God's authority over past and future. Naturally, our sin nature fights against this reality. We are tempted to elevate self, in order that we might perhaps assume a position of authority over life events. From this mindset is birthed a reliving of the past. We believe that we have ultimate control over our decisions and actions rather than seeing God working through life's events to shape us. Or we obsessively try to manipulate the future by incessantly planning. We presume to know the best future and thus strive to obtain it. Yet God clearly states that his purposes will be accomplished. The result is an internal, ultimately futile fight over control. God, at the end of the day, controls our past, present, and future.

Humanistic control stifles one's ability to play. Research on controlling personalities affirms their deformative effect on one's life: "Many authors [in the social and behavioral sciences] point out that the excessive control, as well as the lack of control, or even the illusion of control leads to the impoverishment of the emotional life of the person, deformation of his relations with others, psychological and emotional maladjustment" (Shkurko 2013, 630). In other words, our attempts at control, albeit vain, deplete and damage our emotional health. Emotional depletion impacts our ability to enjoy life.

Imagine some friends are playing a card game. They are enjoying the interaction with one another. The outcome of the game is immaterial, as they are simply delighting in each other's company around a casual game of hearts. You pull up a seat. Instead of joining the game, you decide to control it. You insist that winning should be the goal. Furthermore, you believe laughing should be kept at a minimum so that players can concentrate on strategy to outwit their opponents. Immediately, the tenor of the game would change. Not only would the enjoyment of the other players be muted but it would also be very difficult for you to match their playful attitude, due to your obsession with controlling the manner and outcome of the game.

Play is *the God-given ability and permission to fully enjoy moments in life as God intended, with freedom and pleasure.* Controlling life does not produce freedom or pleasure; rather, it leads to impoverishment and deformation of one's relations with others. Freedom and pleasure arise when we can simply play within the moment. From a theological standpoint, this perspective is grounded in a conviction that we should live life responsibly with wisdom, care, and planning, while fully resting in God's sovereign authority and providence over time.

Honestly, this is not an easy affirmation. And, most certainly, it is not going to be a common one. Yet, it is necessary to move toward this perspective if we are going to *truly be and thus play in the moment.*

THE SABBATH

There are numerous reasons for the Sabbath. Preeminently, it is a day dedicated to honor the Lord (Exod. 20:10–11). As an expression of this honor, humans were instructed to refrain from work; it is a day to rest. Further, the Sabbath was established to safeguard against our human tendency for workaholism. The Sabbath forces us to take a break. It is divine invitation for rest (Gallagher 2019).

Relevant to this chapter, the Sabbath, if truly embraced, can serve as an antidote to our controlling nature. It forces us to be in the moment, even if only for a day. Granted, this requires physical and emotional acceptance. It is possible to physically rest while simultaneously being in a state of emotional unrest. Our minds and hearts continue to process the past or strategize for the future. To holistically embrace the Sabbath necessitates trusting God. This day is an opportunity to surrender, even if for a moment, our need to control life. Ceasing from work and activity as much as possible can force us to recognize that God is ultimately in control rather than us. And honoring the Sabbath should cause us to affirm our dependency upon him.

It is not natural to relinquish control. It requires constant self-reminding. And it cannot be done simply by practicing rest. The Pharisees imposed rest on the Sabbath yet remained fully in control by legislating behavior (Matt. 12:1–8). Relinquishing control involves being *satisfied in the moment in the knowledge that God is orchestrating his purposes in our lives.* Abiding in this truth can be one of the most helpful things for a person's soul. Perhaps by doing so, we can more quickly release anxieties and regrets by affirming the following truths:

> God, you are not surprised by anything that happened yesterday.
>   You are not anxious about what might unfold tomorrow.
> You bring good from every moment in the past,
>   and you see clearly into future troubles.
> Lord, help me to rest in your security,
>   and remain present in today's provision.
> For your grace is sufficient for the moment,
>   and your peace available for the day.

God delights when we rest in the moment. God finds pleasure when we are able to *be*. In *being* we embody a deep trust in him. In *being* we affirm his divine care and providence for our lives. In *being* worship is expressed by acknowledging his sovereign care. Being demonstrates a confident faith in his character. It affirms and receives his love for us. God smiles when we can simply *be* because it communicates to him our contentedness in him and him alone.

Imagine a toddler completely at rest in her mother's arms. She is awake yet not fidgety. She is looking around at life with a quiet contentment, knowing that she is safe in her mother's arms. There is a security reflected in that moment. There is a confidence in her mother's protection and care. The ability to be reflects a trust. As Augustine stated in his *Confessions*, "You made us for yourself, and our heart is restless until it rests in you" (Augustine 1960, 1).

Ultimately, true rest is found in Christ. In Hebrews 3:12–4:13, the author locates rest not in a physical state but in a spiritual relationship with Jesus. The Sabbath was therefore redefined from a specific day to a state of spiritual redemption in our Savior. "So then, there remains a Sabbath rest for the people of God, for whoever has entered God's rest has also rested from his works as God did from his. Let us therefore strive to enter that rest, so that no one may fall by the same sort of disobedience" (Heb. 4:9–11). Truly giving up control is only possible through the work of Christ in our lives; otherwise, our natural human impulses for control will continue to surface.

The trust implicit in the biblical idea of Sabbath connects to play in a powerful way. Genuine play is an active form of being. It is a demonstration that we are OK, even for a moment, with the uncertainty around us. There is a life contentment expressed in play. God-centered play is an affirmation that we can confidently enjoy a moment in life because God is at work around us and in us through Christ. It is an expression of trust in the Creator.

When play is connected to God's sovereignty and redemption, it becomes more than a human moment of enjoyment. It becomes a response to God's loving care, grace, and control. It enables us to have permission to enjoy life because God delights in our being, which can be expressed through play. It can even be worshipful, in that our play is an affirmation that God is sustaining and holding us in that moment. Personally, it should cause us to humbly smile because we have a God who is in essence saying, "You can be still and enjoy this moment because I am overseeing your life."

PLAY AND COMMUNITY

Attempting to control life not only prevents one from playing, it also hinders others' ability to play. Life is lived in community, not isolation. When we are consumed with anxiety, we impact those around us. We have each encountered someone who constantly worries about the future. It is challenging to lift that person up. We might recommend an evening out with the hopes of encouraging that person. If they continue to remain in a state of agitation about the unknown, particularly verbalizing that stress, it suffocates the moment.

Equally, a person who attempts to control life's events stifles another person's freedom. As stated, play comprises a *God-given ability and permission to fully enjoy moments in life as God intended, with freedom and pleasure*. This implies giving others permission to enjoy life with freedom and pleasure. As image bearers of God, it is our responsibility to cultivate conditions of play for others. Controlling another person's moments in life chokes their freedom and thus pleasure. Determining another person's expression of play or preventing that person from playing altogether dehumanizes another person by denying them their God-given freedom. To truly honor this person, we need to create space for that person to play. To do so might even require us to enter their moment of play as an affirmation of our relationship.

The Bible is filled with passages that encourage honor and love toward one another (Luke 6:31; John 13:35; Rom. 12:10). Honor not only involves esteem, it also provides space for that person to thrive. Love is expressed in seeing the needs of another person and striving to satisfy those needs. It is sacrificial. It is others-focused. It is uplifting. First Thessalonians 5:11 reads, "Therefore encourage one another and build one another up." At times, building up another person involves speaking hope into that person. It is pointing that person to Christ. Other times, it involves creating space for that individual to be lifted up. Play can lift us up. Play can release emotional frustration and depression by stirring pleasure in us. Play allows us to experience a moment of goodness and freedom. Granting the ability to play to another person is a form of honor and love.

Play consists of being fully present with oneself so that we can be fully present *with* another person and *for* another person. It is a gift to that person and ultimately to oneself, in that it upholds life-giving community. Allowing that person to have freedom to play—to fully be able to experience those moments—is an expression of love. I indicated this is a hard chapter for me. That is in large part because I have a controlling side to me. I tend to heavily structure my day, which ripples into other people's days, specifically those closest to me. I am asking God to work in this area. Since January 2022, I have been praying daily that I can be more present in the moment so that others can be more present in their moments. In no capacity am I inflating my authority over another person's schedule but rather acknowledging that my approach to life does, in fact, impact those closest to me. Therefore, I need to see play as a community endeavor, not an individual one.

A BRAZILIAN LESSON

In the summer of 2022, my family and I traveled to Brazil. I taught a doctor of ministry course there for several days at a seminary. Then I joined my family for some sightseeing. We had a marvelous time seeing some beautiful sights and enjoying some marvelous food. One of the most refreshing experiences during our time was eating at restaurants. It was not simply the food (which was amazing) but the freedom we had to fully enjoy those moments.

One specific evening stands out to me. It was the second full night we were together. After a long day of sightseeing, we were eager to enjoy an authentic Brazilian steak house. Based on the recommendation of our Uber driver, we went to an intimate place called Bendito. The reason Brazilian restaurants are so refreshing to me is that you are never rushed. When you sit down for the evening, you are there for as long as you want. They truly want you to enjoy the experience. This contrasts sharply with the American perspective, which views your table from a financial standpoint: the longer you remain, the less money the restaurant makes. (This was communicated to us immediately upon our return from Brazil when we made a reservation for our anniversary. The host said, "We can provide a table for 90 minutes but after that you would need to leave because someone else will need use of it.") At Bendito, we could stay as long as we wanted. We ended up staying for three hours. We sat down and looked at the menu. No one came to our table asking us if we needed something. When we were ready to order, we motioned to the waiter and he came over and helped us. After he brought the food, he only came by a couple of times to see if we needed anything. Otherwise, he allowed us to enjoy the food and each other's company. We savored the food. We reminisced over the day's events. We laughed. And we played. We were in that moment, fully enjoying a different country. Time slipped away. Conversation happened naturally. We were *being*. After we finished our food, the waiter came by and quietly picked up our plates, but there was no hint that it was time to go. Not until we motioned to have the check brought to us did the waiter come over and cash us out. It is a memory we will always cherish.

This experience with my family captures the essence of playing in the moment. We were not reliving the past or worrying about the future. We were enjoying a moment of life around food. We were celebrating life. We were thankful for life. Yet, it was not simply up to us. The restaurant gifted us with the time and space to enjoy that moment. We were not concerned about the clock because the restaurant was not concerned about the clock. We were not worried about taking up a table because the culture valued the eating experience. In other words, we were able to play because someone allowed us to play.

ENJOY SOME MINI-SABBATHS

In some respects, play is a mini-Sabbath. It is a moment of rest during the day. It is an opportunity, even for a brief time, to affirm God's sovereignty by releasing the past and the future. Play can offer us physical and emotional rest. It can allow us to truly be. And when we create space for another person to play, we are allowing that person to be.

I would like to offer a practical reminder about learning to be and thus playing in the moment. Some see play as active—for example, playing a sport with others. For others, it is expressed quietly by taking a walk to enjoy God's creation. Play can involve a hobby, such as dancing or sailing. Or it can consist of planting flowers or seeds in one's garden. Playing is less about the activity and more about the state of being at rest under the sovereignty of God. Therefore, it is not possible to provide practical "to dos" as to how to be. This would defeat the purpose. Rather, it involves rediscovering play, then regularly practicing it.

SUMMARIZING THOUGHTS

In its essence, play has an active connotation. It involves doing something. Thus, it is ironic that by playing we are at rest and thus can truly be. Playing is an affirmation of trust—that God is sovereignly at work so that we do not have to be at work and can instead be in the moment. Playing frees us from the bondage of the past and the anxieties of the future. It provides an opportunity to release our controlling tendencies and thoughts to the one who wants us to enjoy life. God delights when we play. He is a Father who finds great pleasure when his children laugh and smile in response to the security and stability he provides.

REFLECTION

As you reflect on this chapter, think about how you play. In what moments do you find true pleasure and freedom? And what is preventing you from stepping into those moments on a regular basis?

1. What is prompting you to control life? Is there an insecurity that causes you to worry about the unknown? Is there a humanistic impulse that wants to have authority over life? It is important to identify the reason why you feel the need for control if you are to truly play.

2. Is your trust in God's sovereignty increasing throughout your life? Do you truly believe he holds the past, present, and future in his hands?

3. Do you regularly practice a Sabbath? Why or why not?

4. Are you resting when you play? What is preventing you from doing so?

5. Are you fully present when you play? We are oftentimes distracted when we play because we are thinking about something else. The next time you play, strive to be fully in the moment.

CHAPTER 5

Learning to Enjoy Life: Playing Requires Permission

It is a happy talent to know how to play.
—Ralph Waldo Emerson

Life has become too squeezed. There was a time when margin existed in our lives. A person could casually relax at work or at home without the gnawing compulsion to do more. In recent years, there has been a rise in calls for work-life balance. Yet, in the post COVID-19 era, it seems that this balance is eroding due to the incessant pull for additional work hours and further commitments at home. Working remotely forever changed the expectation for employees to be accessible after normal business hours. It is now common for employees to log on to work for an hour or two in the evening. For many, this is necessary to keep up with other employees at work who also are working after hours. And thus, the rat race continues.

Equally, at home there is a compulsion to max out extracurricular pursuits. Children are enrolled in activities that consume every day of the week. This is partially a result of parents feeling inferior for not doing so. To pad one's college application, high schoolers are increasingly committing to countless clubs and sports. No one wants to look lazy on their college application. Empty nesters are restless; therefore, they engage in numerous activities, sometimes to fill the identity void created when their children left home. Seniors do not want to be identified as lifeless; therefore, they gather in book clubs and take weekend trips.

For many in our society, less is not more. Duty and obligation have become the mantra at work. And busyness is the default mode at home. The result is a squeezing of any free moment to play. And, more so, play can become neglected because we feel irresponsible when we enjoy playful moments in life, like it shouldn't be a priority.

THE NEED FOR BALANCE

There is a time to work, and there is a time to play. There are times to be serious and times to enjoy life. Ecclesiastes 3:1–4 states,

> For everything there is a season, and a time for every matter under heaven:
> a time to be born, and a time to die;
> a time to plant, and a time to pluck up what is planted;
> a time to kill, and a time to heal;
> a time to break down, and a time to build up;
> a time to weep, and a time to laugh;
> a time to mourn, and a time to dance.

Solomon wrote that there is a time to plant (to work) and a time to laugh (to play). It is essential to maintain this rhythm in life. Life fixated on work leads to humanism; life fixated on pleasure leads to hedonism. It is necessary to cultivate a balance that is healthy for one's soul and relationship with God.

Later in this passage, the author wrote,

> What gain has the worker from his toil? I have seen the business that God has given to the children of man to be busy with. He has made everything beautiful in its time. Also, he has put eternity into man's heart, yet so that he cannot find out what God has done from the beginning to the end. I perceived that there is nothing better for them than to be joyful and to do good as long as they live; also that everyone should eat and

drink and take pleasure in all his toil—this is God's gift to man.
(Eccl. 3:9–13)

The opening question in this section points to a statement that reoccurs throughout Ecclesiastes. Life is "vanity" or "meaningless" (NIV); thus, what benefit is there in work (1:2, 14; 2:17, 19)? In other words, what is the benefit of incessant working in life, without margin or even a breath? Solomon further mused that working is required post-Fall; it is a component of the curse (3:10; Gen. 3:17–19). In time, creation will be redeemed, thus freeing us from the sinful distortions of work (3:11). And even though he has placed "eternity into man's heart" (a longing after him), God's ultimate purposes remain hidden from us. In other words, the author is describing the human condition under the travails of work, duty, and obligation, which are meaningless *without a proper Christian worldview*—since they are not the end goal of life.

Yet, amid this despair, we are encouraged to enjoy life—"to be joyful" and to "eat and drink and take pleasure in all [our] toil" (3:12–13). In other words, it is necessary to push back the chair from work responsibilities and home commitments and enjoy life. In essence, it is necessary to play. It is the counterbalance to duty and obligation, particularly in this sinful world that compels us to do more.

HISTORY'S LESSON

Church history is filled with encouragements to enjoy life. Martin Luther stated, "God is repelled by sorrow of spirit; he hates sorrowful teaching and sorrowful thoughts and words. He takes pleasure in happiness. For he came to refresh us, not to sadden us" (quoted in Potkay 2006, 46). God himself experiences pleasure, and thus it is logical that he would want us to experience the same. Godly pleasure is an expression of bearing his image. Experiencing pleasure in a manner that honors God allows us to experience the happiness of God.

Augustine stated, "If you find physical pleasure in earthy experiences, use the occasion to praise God for these gifts" (2005, 62). He further stated that the focus should not be ultimately on pleasure but rather on the giver, who allows us to enjoy such pleasures. Godly play interweaves pleasure with the divine rather than being simply a human activity.

Thomas Aquinas went further by arguing that play was intended to bring us pleasure so that our souls could be refreshed. In the *Summa Theologiae*, he referred to this as the virtue of *eutrapelia*, or the virtue of "pleasantness of playfulness" (Kress 2012, 1). He stated that games (formal play) have the capacity to restore our soul. He argued that our "souls take rest in a kind of pleasure" (Kress 2012, 1). In other words, play can be uplifting for both our physical bodies and our spirits. It has the effect of lightening us—allowing us to see the good in life and, therefore, to be able to enjoy it.

Pleasure should not be viewed in opposition to the Christian faith but as an expression of it. At times, Christian communities view spiritual disciplines—prayer, fasting, and meditation—as the only means to spiritual growth. These disciplines thus become viewed as forms of duty and obligation. Over time, this emphasis on the contemplative, internal life can lead to seriousness. While these disciplines are good and profitable, they should be balanced with playfulness and pleasure.

When play is detached from our spiritual development, it quickly becomes relegated to the human plane. It is enjoyable but not spiritual. And thus arises the Christian tendency to view play as entertainment rather than profitable for our souls. Because we do not have a robust theology of play, it becomes enticing to embrace the worldly form of play—that which solely seeks one's own pleasure. If our expressions of pleasure are not grounded in a biblical worldview, we will not be able to discern adequately how to play in such a way that brings pleasure not only to our souls but also to God. By cultivating a rich theology of play, Christians are not only able to discern what is God-honoring play but to *fully enjoy moments in life with freedom and pleasure.*

GIVE YOURSELF PERMISSION TO PLAY

As stated in the previous chapter, productivity is defined in terms of something tangible. It involves completion of tasks or projects. It is not uncommon for me to assess the success of the day based on things accomplished. There is a sense of satisfaction in completing things. So I find it difficult to see play in the realm of the productive. Yet, it can be, and it should be.

The fall of 2022 was particularly beautiful as the leaves changed colors. Pennsylvania autumns can be gorgeous. The previous few years I had failed to fully enjoy them due to a busy teaching schedule. It was not uncommon for me to barely notice the array of colors as I fixated on a computer screen or a lesson plan. That year I committed to taking in the season richly and deeply. The last weekend in October, I recommended to my wife that we visit a forested area near our house called Middle Creek. We had the afternoon free, and the weather forecast was for low 60s and sun. It also happened to be the weekend predicted to be the peak time for color.

We put on our boots, grabbed cups of coffee, and headed to the forest. We parked the car and chose a trail that we had never hiked before. Immediately, the array of colors took our breath away. With little rain the previous week, the leaves were still clinging to the branches. A light breeze would have knocked them to the ground. Yet they stood motionless, providing a thick canopy above us. The mixture of greens, reds, yellows, and browns, sometimes on the same tree, prompted spontaneous praises that "God is so creative and good." The light shining through the leaves created a kaleidoscope of hues. As we walked, the leaves that had fallen crunched beneath our boots. With every turn on the trail, the richness of the autumn forest enveloped us. Halfway through the hike was a vista looking out over a lake below. Picturesque trees lined the lake with geese frolicking on the water's edge. It was idyllic and serene.

With each step, I found my heart becoming lighter and more refreshed. The worries of the previous week dissipated into the recesses of my mind. The concerns and burdens of decisions made and ones still to be made disappeared in this rapturous moment of enjoying God's creation. As I stepped emotionally into this moment, my heart slowly moved from enjoyment to praise. This moment of pleasure was both personally enriching and spiritually edifying. I not only found myself stopping and being present in the moment, I longed to remain there—to be still and savor.

This is the power of play. It can move us past a human experience to one that is spiritual. It can refresh our hearts and our souls. The pleasure itself can move us beyond being admirers of God's creativity to experiencers of God's pleasure. For in that moment, as we sat still and delighted in God's creation, I believe we experienced God's pleasure in his own creation. Play became an encounter with the divine.

There were countless "productive" things I could have done that day. I could have attended to some much-needed house projects. I could have caught up on emails. I could have taken time for a longer devotion. Those things would have provided the tangible checks to a "successful" day. Yet they would not have been nearly as productive or successful as the hike in the forest. Productivity was being present in the moment, playing in the midst of God's creation. It proved to be the most successful, meaningful thing I did that day. I only needed to give myself permission to play.

REFRAMING PERMISSION TO PLAY THEOLOGICALLY

What does permission look like theologically? To embrace play, we need to see it as good for us. It rests in the truth that God loves to give us good things, to build us up. It is not a deviation from our spiritual responsibilities but rather an expression of them. I believe God hardwired us to play. One small example is the uniqueness of humans' ability to laugh. No other animal has the capacity to laugh in response to a joke. Hyenas laugh but not in response to enjoyment; it is due to high stress—a defense mechanism. Humans laugh because we are enjoying a moment in life. It is an expression of our uniqueness as image bearers.

To grant ourselves permission to play, we need a theological infusion into our understanding of play. It is necessary to see it as more than a means of entertainment and pleasure, as something that is spiritually good and meaningful for us. This involves seeing play through the lens of God. It then moves from optional to necessary.

Play Is Spiritually Good for Us

James 1:17 states, "Every good gift and every perfect gift is from above, coming down from the Father of lights, with whom there is no variation or shadow due to change." This passage does not define the word *gift*. It simply affirms that God bestows upon us good gifts. The ultimate gift is salvation. However, there are other gifts such as family, vocation, and leisure. God desires that we find fulfillment in family and work. But he also grants us reprieve from the responsibilities of life by giving us the ability to play.

Play is good in that it allows us to connect with others. Play allows us to enjoy God's creation. Play provides human pleasure. Yet it is also true that play has a profound spiritual benefit because it allows us to enjoy the fullness of our humanness by celebrating God's gift of life. Play is *eutrapelia*—it allows our "souls [to] take rest in a kind of pleasure" (Kress 2012, 1). It enables a spiritual wholeness and intrapersonal freedom. I believe there is something obtained in play that is not possible in other forms of human expression and activity. It allows us to taste life's goodness, even briefly. Let's look at some of the spiritual benefits of play.

Play Is Spiritually Life-Giving to Us

Proverbs 17:22 states, "A joyful heart is good medicine, but a crushed spirit dries up the bones." This verse highlights the human benefits of joy: It is medicinal. It is uplifting. It is restorative. In contrast, the latter portion of the verse captures the emotional strain of a crushed spirit: It is stifling and depressing. It suffocates.

Play stirs joy in us. There is a "pleasantness of playfulness" (Kress 2012, 1). It is life-giving. It is restorative. Imagine having a horrible day. Something happened that set you off. It might have been failing a test or a relationship falling apart. Perhaps you received some unwanted news at work. Or a trusted coworker violated your trust. You come home to your family or spouse. After you vent for a moment, your loved one comes over to you, looks you in the eyes, and cracks a joke. They then poke you playfully. As much as you want to be angry, you cannot help but smile and chuckle. In that moment of play, you experience a lightening—some restoration. Play is spiritually life-giving, for in that moment our soul becomes lighter.

Play Is Spiritually Meaningful to Us

Humans are created to connect with others. From the beginning, God deemed it is not good for a human to be alone. It is essential to be in relationships. We long for human connection and belonging. A person can play in isolation. However, many times play involves community. It is an opportunity to interact playfully with others. This human connection is meaningful in that it cultivates in us acceptance and safety. When play is shared with others, there is a human intimacy that is fostered.

Research indicates that experiences grow fonder as one grows older. Amit Kumar stated that experiences "provide more enduring happiness" (Kumar, Killingsworth, and Gilovich 2014, 1924). Even if the memory is not perfect, our mind wants to view it as pleasing. He indicated that the "fleetingness" of these experiences makes them dearer to us. This contrasts with physical gifts that deteriorate over time. As an example, we can hardly remember a specific item given to us as a gift. But we can easily recall a present that involved an experience. Why? Because there was meaning attached to that human connection. That moment of play was not simply about the experience; it was about the meaning. This truth is one reason why my wife and I decided early in our marriage not to give physical presents for birthdays. Rather, we celebrate these moments with playful experiences. We have enjoyed rock climbing, skydiving, baseball games, concerts, and scavenger hunts, to name a few. As we look back at the last twenty-six years, we have a colorful slideshow of playful memories that surface in our minds. It is not primarily the activity that was enjoyable; it was the meaningfulness of those moments with loved ones that brought and continues to bring pleasure. These relationships are spiritual blessings infused with affirmation, safety, and intimacy. Play is an arena to celebrate these blessings.

Play Is Spiritually Therapeutic for Us

There are times when it is necessary to play as a means of emotional health. Play therapy is an increasingly popular field that provides psychological support and assistance to children. In essence, a trained therapist uses play to assist children in identifying and articulating emotions. At times, it involves observation to detect stress and anxiety. Other times, it is a means to create conversations around traumatic events. In sum, play is used among children as a means of psychological healing because play unlocks distress and trauma.

For some reason, this form of therapy is relegated to children. However, is it not also possible that play can have equal benefit for adults? I wonder if some mental health concerns might be alleviated by engaging in play. Is it not possible that play provides opportunities for healing in addition to moments of pleasure?

I believe one reason we do not embrace play is because it is simply viewed as leisure. It is framed around a hobby—a moment to have fun. But if we were to reframe play around emotional, physical, relational, and psychological benefits, we could move it from elective (if I have time) to necessary (this is good for my soul). Perhaps one of the reasons we are not motivated to play more regularly is because we view it as secondary to the more important responsibilities in life—work, church, and ministry.

To summarize play theologically,

- If God wanted us to be more serious, he would have withheld smiles.
- If God wanted us to be more intense, he would have deprived us of sleep.
- If God wanted us to be more efficient, he would have given us greater capacities.
- God wanted us to enjoy life, so he gave us relationships.
- God wanted us to breathe in the fabric of life, so he gave us days off.
- God wanted us to play, so he gave us laughter.

DISCOVER YOUR UNIQUE TYPE OF PLAY LANGUAGE

Gary Chapman authored the popular book *The Five Love Languages*. It wisely presents the unique expressions of love, explaining how everyone receives love in a particular way and, as a result, expresses love uniquely to other people.

The premise of Chapman's book is that humans are unique in that we experience love in specific ways. I am different from my spouse, who is different from our children. This is the beautiful reality of individuals made in God's image. Each person is an individual tapestry in the eyes of God, thus embodying innately personal expressions and affinities.

This truth is germane to the topic of play. While you might share an experience of play with another person, it is quite likely that you will enjoy play differently than that person. In this book, play is defined as *the God-given ability and permission to fully enjoy moments in life as God intended, with freedom and pleasure.* If this is true, I propose that God uniquely created each person to enjoy play in a particular way. In other words, we have preferences as to how we most enjoy play. And when we play in that fashion, we most experience freedom and pleasure. For example, a person might enjoy playing outside by themselves rather than indoors with a group of people. For that person, playing in their preferred setting and manner opens pathways for freedom and pleasure. In contrast, when that same person is asked to play board games inside, while they might have an enjoyable time, it will not be as refreshing and life-giving. This is important to note and learn as we engage in play and interact with others in their form of play.

I did not intentionally mirror Chapman's book; however, I am proposing five types of play language. To structure these types of play languages, I attempted to make them distinct from one another. I also reflected on the human experience to discern whether they are intuitively true. They revolve around relationships, setting, form, structure, and intentionality.

The Play Language of Relationships: Solitary or Communal

Everyone values relationships. However, there is a unique difference when it comes to personality. Extroverts find energy from being with other people; introverts are drained in such settings. Relationships are important to both; however, a person is largely enlivened or not depending on their personality type.

This is true of play. If the purpose of play is to find freedom and pleasure, it makes sense that introverts would prefer a *solitary* form of play. That individual is most energized when they can play in small groups or by themselves. For this person, play is most enjoyed by taking a walk in the park or enjoying a game on one's phone. Or it might consist of an activity only involving one or two people, like the hike my wife and I took. As introverts, we prefer small groups. Would we enjoy hiking with a group of ten individuals? Yes. Would it be as *freeing and pleasurable*? No. Play is most life-giving when it aligns with one's disposition.

In contrast, a person who is extroverted enjoys being in groups. This is my daughter's preference. For Ashleigh, play should be communal. For extroverts, play might involve a game of pickup basketball, a restaurant outing with friends, or a weekend retreat with other couples. For the introverts, a weekend retreat with other couples would be met with a deep sigh, sacrifice, and a great deal of grumbling. Death might be preferable. For the extrovert, it is energizing and enticing. They would enjoy the interaction over meals with other couples. Sharing their lives in conversation and creating new memories with others would be stimulating and refreshing.

One form of play is not better than another. It is simply that we are uniquely wired to experience freedom and pleasure in a specific way. It is possible to enjoy other contexts of play; it is just not as freeing.

The Play Language of Setting: Indoors or Outdoors

Some prefer the indoors; others like the outdoors. If given the opportunity to go to the movies or enjoy an evening stroll, one might choose the former, while others choose the latter. At times, it is simply a matter of mood. Perhaps you are tired and just want to slide into a comfortable chair and be entertained, even if you prefer the outdoors. For others, the choice is based on the movie. If it is a long-anticipated movie, you might choose that option, even if staying indoors is not preferable. And, of course, the temperature matters. I might prefer the outdoors unless it is a Chicago winter (while cold-natured individuals are saying a hearty amen).

In the end, we typically have a disposition when it comes to the setting for play. My son enjoys the outdoors, specifically the night sky. If you asked him, his most preferred setting for play would be outdoors in the evening. He would rather be outside gazing up at the stars than inside bowling. For others, they would prefer to be at the theater rather than outside at a football game. In general, we have a preferred setting for play.

For many, the precise setting matters. I personally experience the most freedom and pleasure when I am near a large body of water. When I say large, I mean ocean rather than a small lake. If I can see the other side, it is too small. Even more so, I love being on that body of water, thus the reason sailing is a truly life-giving form of play for me. My wife, on the other hand, loves the forest. Walking through dense trees with foliage all around immediately lifts her soul. We both enjoy the outdoors; however, specific settings are more freeing, and thus more pleasurable, than others. We joke about retiring in the United States, either in the Northwest or the Northeast, where dense wilderness hugs the ocean. This way we both would be in heaven.

The Form of Play Language: Active or Passive

As you can suspect, I love play that is active. I find great enjoyment in play that is *doing*. The ideal form of play is when I am busy and physically engaged, while at the same time thinking intensely on that play. For me, working on my son's Jeep falls within that camp. Sailing most certainly is in that category. Reading a book is not play to me. Even watching a sporting event on TV does not produce pleasure and freedom in me.

Others find deep enjoyment by relaxing in a hammock, reading a magazine. Or you might love grabbing a Starbucks drink and watching the boats pass by on the beach. For you, this is truly playing because it involves doing nothing and thinking about nothing. You enjoy sitting still and allowing activity to occur around you while your mind enjoys the moment.

One's energy level matters in terms of form. Experiencing a busy week at work and home might prompt you to long for an evening of doing nothing, while under normal circumstances you would rather be adventurous. On the other hand, if you have been confined to a desk all week without interruption, you might want to be active even though your normal tendency is to enjoy a romantic movie curled up on the couch. As you reflect on your own form of play language, it is important to remember what your natural tendency is rather than what you might desire in that instance. Your natural tendency is your true form of play language, not what you might need in the moment.

The Structure of Play Language: Formal or Informal

Some individuals like the theater, concerts, or museums. Others like playing in the leaves, dancing at a restaurant, or biking. Individuals typically fall somewhere on the continuum between formal activities and informal ones. Depending on the moment, you could land in either camp. If you are in New York, you might enjoy going to the Metropolitan Museum of Art. Or, on that same trip, a bike ride through Central Park sounds delightful. However, it is likely that true freedom and pleasure is found on one side or the other.

For others, the formal and informal can be extended beyond an event to a general rhythm in life. In other words, you might want play to be routine and consistent. When we lived in Chicago, my wife and I had season tickets to Drury Lane, a local theater. This routine was helpful for us as young parents. During the busyness of this time, it guaranteed that we had five evenings out a year to play as a couple. It was life-giving to us because we had something to look forward to. The informal likely would not have happened during this season of life. However, our natural desire is for variety. Since moving to Lancaster, Pennsylvania, we have always been looking for different things to do in the area, striving to find new experiences. Others joke to us that we have done more in the area than those who have lived there for fifty years. For us, variety is preferred and thus more enjoyable.

This doesn't suggest a person can't appreciate other types of play; it just means everyone enjoys pleasure and freedom more pronouncedly within certain spheres. It is necessary to play, even if it requires adopting a structure that is not entirely freeing to you. But when given the opportunity to choose the structure, it would be beneficial if you played often in the manner that refreshes you the most.

The Intentionality of Play: Planned or Spontaneous

Intentionality has some carryover from structure, yet there are some distinctions. An act of play can be formal yet spontaneous. You might come home one evening and spontaneously choose to go to a concert. The event is formal, yet the intentionality is spontaneous. Conversely, one might plan several weeks in advance to go to the beach for the day with the intent of simply playing in the sand with no specific agenda. It is planned yet informal.

For those who are planners, this can sometimes serve as the means to play once that event arrives. I enjoy planning our family vacations. Months in advance of the trip, I chart out various sights to see, routes to take, and restaurants to check out. I typically have a detailed itinerary that describes the activities and even their order prior to arriving at our vacation destination. For some, this might seem to take the enjoyment out of vacation. Where is the spontaneity? For me, I plan so that I can play. I do not want to think about maps, routes, and looking up sights while away. I want to be fully present, enjoying the moment. For me, planning is critical to playing. For others, this level of planning would be the death of play. Where is the adventure? Where is the spontaneous decision to go check out something new? Each person should know where they fall on the continuum of intentionality.

Bringing Play Languages Together

These five expressions are not to be viewed as mutually exclusive. They should be placed on continuums. Every person lands somewhere on each of the five areas. For example, someone might prefer a planned, informal, outdoor event that is communal and active. Someone else might desire a spontaneous, formal, indoor experience that is also communal and active. They reflect different types of play, but to those specific individuals they are freeing and pleasurable.

It is important to discover your own expression of play. This will enable you to identify the activities and manner by which to *enjoy moments in life, with freedom and pleasure*. Furthermore, it will enable you to give yourself permission to play, since that play will be attractive and life-giving to you. In other words, you will want to play because it aligns with how God uniquely created you.

It is also important to discover the type of play language of those closest to you—spouses, family, and friends. Play is likely different for the other person. Yet the natural tendency when we think of play is to imagine it in the form most attractive to ourselves. But in relationships where we are called to love and sacrifice, it is essential to not only know the other person's play expressions but also to embrace them. Loving that person involves *playing for the good of the other*. This means embracing the play that is most life-giving to the other person. For example, I know my wife loves forests, whereas I enjoy large bodies of water. While in Chicago, there were times she would go on the sailboat with me even though the water made her anxious. It wasn't as freeing and pleasurable to her as to me, but she embraced it because she knew it was life-giving to me. Equally, I love to suggest a hike in the wilderness because it is a deep form of play for her. In relationships, it is important to find common ground when it comes to play, but it is also essential to sacrifice for the other person.

Understanding your own type of play language and those of others is critical. In its absence, we very well could be shaped by others' ideals of play. Others might be more persistent on an expression of play; therefore, we go along with it. Or maybe their idea seems more exciting. For example, it looks like so much fun to go to the club and dance with a group of people. Therefore, you go, only to find yourself exhausted at the end of the evening, never having truly played. Sometimes, we don't truly play because we are being molded by others' play languages rather than embracing our own.

There are also specific considerations when it comes to play. In some instances, play is for fun, whereas other times it serves as therapy. It is important in such instances to know that play for therapy might be a momentary need rather than an affirmation of your play language. It might be necessary to be with friends after a difficult day at school or work even though you normally would prefer to be alone. The circumstances in such cases might dictate the most beneficial form of play in that moment. For others, a difficult day might require taking thirty minutes to process through the anxieties and stress of work to be able to be present in the play. Otherwise, you might be *playing but not fully enjoying the play* because your mind is still at work. In other words, what happens prior to play can determine one's ability to play.

Psalm 139:13–14 states,

> For you formed my inward parts;
>   you knitted me together in my mother's womb.
> I praise you, for I am fearfully and wonderfully made.

God created us beautifully, wonderfully, and *uniquely*. This includes the way we like to play. Everyone is different in how they play. Some enjoy outdoors; some enjoy formal activities. Some enjoy spontaneous events; some more structure. Some are introverts, and some are extroverts. Humanity is amazing in all its splendor, and this includes the arena of play.

NEXT STEPS

In terms of next steps, I would like to offer four practical recommendations. First, it might be important to schedule play at first. If play has become a foreign aspect in your life, it is necessary to simply step into it. But if it is not natural or integrated into a daily or weekly routine, sitting down with a calendar and carving out times to play might be useful as an initial step.

Second, as it becomes more regular in your life, you can begin to experiment with various expressions of play. Whereas God knows your unique expressions of play, you might yet have to discover them. As is true with other skills and talents, you will not know how you have been formed unless you try things out in life. As you embrace certain play languages, the ones that are most life-giving, freedom inspiring, and pleasurable will become known to you.

Third, it might be necessary to redeem your form of play. It is possible your play expressions are not aligned with a Christian ethic. The reason might be because you have been allured by the world's play, or your play has been molded by others, namely, non-Christians. If this is the case, ask God for wisdom as to how to uphold play in a way that is godly.

Finally, play might require disconnecting from the world, particularly social media. Discerning how God uniquely wired you involves listening to the quiet voice of the Holy Spirit. In these moments, you can see God's wisdom and direction. Furthermore, play is a mindset. It is best done when the mind is less cluttered. To fully play sometimes requires dealing with personal baggage to position oneself to fully enjoy play. We will discuss personal baggage more in chapter 7.

SUMMARIZING THOUGHTS

In our fast-paced, hectic world, it can be difficult to play. Play can be seen as unproductive. Yet it is necessary to embrace play for our spiritual edification and enjoyment. To do so requires giving oneself permission to play. Essential to stepping into play is seeing it as connected and beneficial to one's spiritual life and recognizing that God fashioned us uniquely with play languages. When embraced, our particular type of play language leads us into a life of enjoyment with freedom and pleasure.

REFLECTION

As you reflect on this chapter, think about your unique form of play. How has God wired you? What play expressions give you the most freedom and pleasure?

1. Are you giving yourself permission to play? Sometimes we feel guilty for playing because it seems unproductive. Yet play is incredibly productive, both spiritually and emotionally.

2. Do you see play as having a spiritual component? Do you see it as a necessary spiritual discipline? Begin to pray about connecting play to your spiritual life.

3. What are your unique expressions of play? Experiment with play languages this month to better discern how God has uniquely created you.

4. Do you know the unique play languages of those around you? Are you creating space for those individuals to truly play?

5. Take a moment several times this week and step into play. It might involve scheduling it so that you become accustomed to it. In time, it will become more natural.

Learning to Appreciate the World: Playing in Culture

Culture arises and unfolds in and as play.
—Johan Huizinga

We live in a multicultural world—a beautiful kaleidoscope created and sustained by God. The previous chapter explored individual play languages. At face value, this can easily be interpreted as play viewed from a Western perspective. This is a fair assessment. I did propose *individual* expressions, which gives an air of Western individualism. Since I am a Westerner, it is understandable that I would present this topic through my own cultural grid. While the theological foundations of each chapter transcend culture, there are naturally some cultural expressions embedded throughout the book.

This chapter serves to compliment chapter 5 by affirming the universal phenomenon of play. Play is embedded in every culture and is a gift given by God to all humanity. In fact, play is not simply reserved for humans, as it is also present in the animal kingdom, visible when dolphins jump in the wake of a boat or a dog fetches a stuffed animal. Play is *integrated* into the fabric of God's creation, regardless of one's ethnic particularity. Play is also *expressed* in every culture. While there are forms of play that transcend cultures, such as the Olympic sports, cultures often have unique cultural expressions. The Adumu dance of the Maasai people of Kenya and the traditional Japanese kite festival epitomize this. There are even culturally specific games, such as the Arabic game mancala. One of the beautiful benefits of a global world is the accessibility of cultural forms of play. It allows us to celebrate God's creativity within cultures.

This chapter seeks to ground cultural expressions in God. This is essential to a theology of play that embraces cultural particularities. If culture is simply an evolutionary by-product of human migration, cultural forms of play are only illustrative. We can provide examples from different cultures but nothing more. However, if cultural variety and expressions are part of God's purposes, it has theological benefit to us. It becomes his gift to us. And specifically, if play is culturally embedded and expressed, seeing forms of play in context also has benefit beyond simple entertainment. It can inform us of God's diverse world and design, and more so, about God himself.

GOD CREATED ETHNIC DIVERSITY

The early pages of Genesis detail God's desire for multiplication. Genesis 1:28 states, "And God blessed them [male and female]. And God said to them, 'Be fruitful and multiply and fill the earth and subdue it, and have dominion over the fish of the sea and over the birds of the heavens and over every living thing that moves on the earth.'" This command is reiterated in Genesis 9:7, "And you, be fruitful and multiply, increase greatly on the earth and multiply in it."

On the heels of this command, we find the account of the tower of Babel, chronicling the scattering of nations and confusion of languages (Gen. 11:1–9).

> Now the whole earth had one language and the same words. And as people migrated from the east, they found a plain in the land of Shinar and settled there. And they said to one another, "Come, let us make bricks, and burn them thoroughly." And they had brick for stone, and bitumen for mortar. Then they said, "Come, let us build ourselves a city and a tower with its top in the heavens, and let us make a

name for ourselves, lest we be dispersed over the face of the whole earth." And the LORD came down to see the city and the tower, which the children of man had built. And the LORD said, "Behold, they are one people, and they have all one language, and this is only the beginning of what they will do. And nothing that they propose to do will now be impossible for them. Come, let us go down and there confuse their language, so that they may not understand one another's speech." So the LORD dispersed them from there over the face of all the earth, and they left off building the city. Therefore its name was called Babel, because there the LORD confused the language of all the earth. And from there the LORD dispersed them over the face of all the earth.

A careful reading of the passage reveals two important conclusions. First, sinful attitudes and actions of pride prevented the scattering of nations as *God intended*. "Come, let us build ourselves a city and a tower with its top in the heavens, and let us make a name for ourselves, *lest we be dispersed* over the face of the whole earth" (Gen. 11:4). God always intended for humans to "fill the earth" (Gen. 1:28; 9:7); human pride was preventing it. Second, the infusion of new languages provided the impetus to scatter the nations. "Come, let us go down and there confuse their language, so that they may not understand one another's speech. So the LORD *dispersed them* from there over the face of all the earth" (Gen. 11:7–8). God initiated linguistic diversity to accomplish his original purpose to populate the earth.

In addition, Genesis 10 describes the formation of ethnic enclaves, as people groups are spread out into their territories "by their clans, their languages, their lands, and their nations" (Gen. 10:20, 31; see also 10:4). This passage is located prior to the tower of Babel narrative to clearly highlight the fulfillment of Genesis 1 and 9. However, chronologically, it occurs after Genesis 11, in response to the scattering of people (Sung 2011, 259–68). God intended for humans to "fill the earth." The fulfillment began to occur after God scattered the nations, giving rise to ethnic communities. God always desired ethnic diversity.

When it comes to the New Testament, there appears to be some debate as to whether ethnicity should still be promoted. Paul's letters appear to imply the abolishment of gender and race, thus contesting ethnic expressions. Galatians 3:28 states, "There is neither Jew nor Greek, there is neither slave nor free, there is no male and female, for you are all one in Christ Jesus." At first glance, this verse seems to imply that individuals are ethnicity-free once they embrace their new identity in Christ. This interpretation misunderstands the passage. The purpose is to highlight the reduction of ethnic identities and barriers for the unifying nature of Jesus Christ. The gender and ethnicity statements "do not mean that all male-female distinctions" have been eliminated "in Christ, any more than there is not racial difference between the Christian Jew and the Christian Gentile" (Fung 1988, 175; Campbell 2008, 147). Rather, the redemption of Jesus Christ liberates sinful expressions that historically have accompanied lived realities of gender or ethnicity.

Reinforcing this sentiment, Colossians 3:11 states, "Here there is not Greek and Jew, circumcised and uncircumcised, barbarian, Scythian, slave, free; but Christ is all, and in all." Peter O'Brien concluded that this verse emphasizes an abolishment of sinful influences, "the barriers that divided people from one another—racial, religious, cultural and social" (1982, 192). The emphasis is on the sinful results arising from ethnic group interaction, not the nature of ethnicity itself.

It is essential to maintain theological coherence and consistency when exploring biblical themes. If we acknowledge a gender aspect within personhood, as articulated in Scripture, "So God created man in his own image, in the image of God he created him; male and female he created them" (Gen. 1:27), we must also acknowledge an ethnicity aspect as well, since gender and ethnicity are parallel in the New Testament passages in Galatians and Colossians. In other words, we cannot say that ethnicity should be dismissed based on these passages when we clearly would not state that gender no longer exists. Therefore, God has a purpose for ethnic diversity. In addition, the language and purpose of Genesis 11 supports a divine commissioning of ethnic scattering in the world. The redemptive work in Jesus Christ does not abolish this decree but rather gives it a divinely restored expression: diversity is fully realized in Christ.

In addition, the eschatological reality includes ethnic distinctions. Revelation 7:9–10 states,

> After this I looked, and behold, a great multitude that no one could number, from every nation, from all tribes and peoples and languages, standing before the throne and before the Lamb, clothed in white robes, with palm branches in their hands, and crying out with a loud voice, "Salvation belongs to our God who sits on the throne, and to the Lamb!"

Tribal distinctions and language diversity are present in heaven. In glory, God has preserved and upheld ethnic diversity. Yet sin is no longer present; therefore, heaven will reflect perfect multicultural harmony, fully embodying our glorified state with persons from all ethnic communities.

Furthermore, there are nations in the New Jerusalem. Revelation 21:24–26 provides another glimpse into heaven:

> By its light will the nations walk, and the kings of the earth will bring their glory into it, and its gates will never be shut by day—and there will be no night there. They will bring into it the glory and the honor of the nations.

Interestingly, a few verses later, the tree of life is for the "healing of the nations" (22:2), giving credence to the biblical interpretation that ethnic expression is embraced by God, with ethnic discord being a result of the curse (22:2–3). Jesus invites all people (thus, all "cultures") to himself, creating a new life-giving relationship (Jennings 2010, 266, 273). The result is freedom that leads to cultural expression and validation (Jennings 2010, 288). This will be fully realized in heaven when sin is absent, as we authentically worship God with our unique cultural expressions.

These passages demonstrate God's plan and desire for ethnic diversity and cultural expressions. They reflect his passion and heart for the world.

They are essential parts of his redemptive story. And they are God's gift to the world to celebrate and enjoy. This is essential to remember in a world that is polarized over race. A robust theology of ethnic diversity serves as an antidote to ethnocentrism (my culture is superior) and theological colonialism (your culture needs rescuing).

HOW DOES ETHNIC DIVERSITY CONNECT TO PLAY?

If ethnic diversity and cultural expressions are a gift from God, then the playful expressions within culture are also a gift. They are to be appreciated, enjoyed, and celebrated. It is tempting in a global world to either dismiss or exotify another culture, including in the realm of play. Cultural dancing is framed as primitive rather than celebrated as an expression of cultural heritage and tradition. I live in Lancaster County, known for its Amish community. It is not uncommon to see Amish children playing in a field with handmade wooden toys. Honestly, my first reaction is sometimes not to honor their playful expression but to view it as quaint, archaic, and exotic. This does not esteem or honor this cultural expression of play.

Equally concerning is an approach that dismisses cultural play. I participated in two mission trips to Romania. On one of my trips, I witnessed a portion of a traditional Romanian wedding while visiting a village. I say a portion because wedding ceremonies typically last several days and nights. They involve expressive dancing in traditional Romanian dress. The entire community participates in the festivities with prescribed foods and folk music. There is even a tradition where the bride is kidnapped by a group of friends late in the evening. She is taken to a club until the groom pays a ransom. Within the playfulness of this wedding ceremony are family customs and village pride. It is not simply the uniting of two individuals but of an entire community.

When I returned from my first mission trip, I became acquainted with several Romanians living in the United States. Two of them got engaged. Since their families still lived in Romania, they returned to their home country for their wedding. However, having been enamored with American culture, they decided to have a traditional US wedding rather than a Romanian one. They insisted that it start promptly at a particular time. To ensure people arrived on time, they announced the wedding time on the invitation as two hours early. The entire wedding ceremony lasted one hour, followed by a short reception. It was an American wedding yet with Romanians in Romania. I am confident the couple enjoyed this day. But I wonder how the community felt. I imagine the families perceived it as lacking in community spirit. I suspect they felt dishonored, as if their cultural play was inferior to that of the West. They likely felt deprived of an opportunity to fully participate in this union with tradition, heritage, and celebration. Their cultural play was dismissed rather than honored. These moments of cultural play are opportunities to appreciate God's multiethnic desires and purpose.

THE BENEFITS OF CULTURAL PLAY

Cultural play is not simply a means of pleasure. It is an expression of localized values, worldview, and community traditions. As such, play is something individuals in every culture choose to engage in voluntarily. It is a natural expression of their society. It involves activities and engagements that provide refreshment and joy in their cultural context, and therefore, serve as true reflections of that culture's heart and soul.

Cultural Play Is an Expression of Values

Geert Hofstede developed an extensive framework for cultural values, exploring areas such as power distance and uncertainty avoidance (Johnson 2021, 371–73). His model attempts to understand the dimensions of individual cultures. The specific value that most relates to play is the individualism versus collectivism spectrum. Certain cultures are more collectivistic. This is reflected in the Romanian example. A wedding is a community affair. It is almost more about the community than the individuals. On the other side of the spectrum are individualistic cultures, such as the United States. A wedding in America is usually entirely about the couple; the community members are largely observers.

Guofang Li stated, "Play is part of the basic developmental experiences of human lives. Children learn about culture, social norms, and language through play" (2017). Play is formative for cultural development. Exploring the relationship between culture and play, Patricia Ramsey stated,

Children's play preferences reflect the values that they're being raised in. Children from a more individualistic culture may prefer to spend time alone. They may prefer to spend time doing competitive activities. They may be more caught up in individual achievement and smaller groups, maybe more exclusionary activities, whereas children raised in a more collective, collaborative culture may emphasize inclusion and play in larger groups and be less concerned with a competitive aspect. (n.d.)

Culture influences play. By the time an individual reaches adulthood, play and culture have become intertwined. Play then becomes an expression of those values. I observed this firsthand through a game I utilize in my doctoral classrooms. It is called Broken Squares. Classes break out into groups of five. Each person in the group receives an envelope with pieces of cutout squares. The pieces are incomplete. To complete a specific square, the individual needs pieces from the other members of the group. The goal is to construct five equally sized squares before the other teams do so, all without speaking or taking pieces. Each person can only give pieces away. The goal of the game is to cultivate collaboration. In the United States, the dynamics are always the same. The groups become very competitive against one another. One or two individuals get frustrated in the group and attempt to take charge. Typically, they start taking pieces from other group members to win the game.

Expecting the same results, I introduced this game to a class I was teaching among leaders in Brazil. The response could not have been more different. They were patient with one another. They were not interested in winning the game. Rather, they were working together, in harmony, without a hint of competitiveness. There was no frustration but rather enjoyment. I was slightly disappointed in that I was hoping to create some tension in the classroom. It was the same game with two different reactions. The manner of the play reflected the cultural values. In Brazil, harmony and collaboration are cherished values. There is a sense of pride in working together. In contrast, the United States encourages individuality and competition.

Following the crossing of the Red Sea as the Israelites were rescued from Egypt, they sang and danced. They honored God for his deliverance. Exodus 15:20–21 states,

> Then Miriam the prophetess, the sister of Aaron, took a tambourine in her hand, and all the women went out after her with tambourines and dancing. And Miriam sang to them:
> "Sing to the LORD, for he has triumphed gloriously;
> the horse and his rider he has thrown into the sea."

We do not know the specifics of the dance; however, I suspect it had a deep cultural flavor. The Israelites had been in bondage for 430 years (Exod. 12:40). At long last, they were free from the oppression of the Egyptians. They were able to now worship God freely. I imagine Miriam saying, "I have been waiting a very long time to honor Yahweh freely and openly." So, she grabbed an instrument and led the women in praise in their own cultural expression, not that of the Egyptians. At the very least, the focus of the dancing was God-honoring, as they sang to the Lord, their deliverer and rescuer.

Cultural Play Shapes Meaning and Beliefs

Cultural play is not simply for cultural expression; it is a mechanism to nurture meaning and beliefs within culture. This begins during childhood. As parents interact with children during play, they are framing those activities and moments through a particular cultural lens (Hyun 1998). In doing so, they are cultivating cultural meaning and beliefs in the child. For example, in the West, autonomy and self-reliance is prized. As such, children are encouraged to interact with toys independently and exploratively. It is a means to independence. Unwittingly, this is shaping the child's understanding and beliefs as "individual independence, self-reliance, self-help, and autonomy are respected and encouraged" (Hyun 1998, 44). Children grow up to value these beliefs. It becomes part of their life perspective. In this sense, play shapes an individual's worldview.

As children grow up, these beliefs become cemented in a person. They become part of each person's identity. In the church I pastored in

Chicago, we had a Hispanic congregation that oftentimes met separately from the main church. In many Latino societies, children are encouraged to roam and play, at times without adult supervision. I visited the Bible studies and worship gatherings on occasion. It was not uncommon for children to be wandering and playing expressively while someone was teaching or leading. The parents were not fazed by this. The culture encouraged this dynamic interaction and flexibility. The cultural clash occurred when the children would attend a children's ministry called Awana. This ministry was structured with children rotating between worship, Bible memorization, and games at precise times. On occasion during these evenings, the Latino children would wander off to another part of the building. We would find them playing separately from the formal activities. For them, this was normal. To others, this was disruptive. It led to numerous conversations about how to maintain order with some accommodation. Culture shaped these children's beliefs, which influenced their practices.

One summer I asked an elder, who was Latino, to lead the annual church picnic. Typically, we would have the event on an afternoon for three hours. It included food and plenty of games. It was a time to fellowship and play. This particular year the elder approached me about changing the overall structure. He proposed the picnic begin at 8 am in the morning and go until late that afternoon. He proposed numerous games throughout the day, including volleyball and cornhole. Lunch would occur sometime between 12 and 3 p.m. Since I asked him to lead this event, I agreed to the plan. It was interesting to hear the concerns of some members of the church. "What time is lunch going to precisely start?" Or, "This is a long day. Don't you think we should trim it back?" "What is the schedule for the day?" I responded by saying, "It is going to be fun. You are welcome to come at any time and stay as long as you are able to." It turned out to be one of the best picnics in years. Some people came and stayed for the whole day. Others came for a few hours. Games would be played and then they would stop. People ventured on walks and others sat and chatted. It was a multicultural day of play. This story reflects how cultural beliefs and meaning shaped in children become embodied in adults. The same dynamic interaction and flexibility present among the children in the earlier example was then embraced and expressed in the adults. Cultural play shapes meaning and beliefs.

God loves cultural diversity. It should be celebrated. There are times, however, when culture takes on an immoral practice. Shortly after the dancing account of Miriam, the Israelites had another episode of play that led to devastating consequences. While in the wilderness, Moses went up on the mountain to receive instructions from God. In his absence, the Israelites built a golden calf to worship (Exod. 32). Idolatry was a common practice in Egypt; therefore, it is not surprising that they would slide back into this cultural ritual. Scripture states,

> And [Aaron] received the gold from their hand and fashioned it with a graving tool and made a golden calf. And they said, "These are your gods, O Israel, who brought you up out of the land of Egypt!" When Aaron saw this, he built an altar before it. And Aaron made a proclamation and said, "Tomorrow shall be a feast to the LORD." And they rose up early the next day and offered burnt offerings and brought peace offerings. And the people sat down to *eat and drink and rose up to play*. (Exod. 32:4–6)

The people played. Yet it was in sharp contrast to the Miriam account. Rather than honoring the Lord, it was an act of defiance. In response, God brought judgment on the people, leading to the death of three thousand men (Exod. 32:28). This account also illustrates how culture shapes meaning and beliefs. The Israelites had lived in Egypt for 430 years. It would have been impossible to fully insulate themselves from Egyptian practices. The individuals spearheading the construction of the golden calf were raised in a culture that embraced idolatry; therefore, to them, it was normal. The meaning and beliefs of the culture had become embedded in their worldview and found expression in their play. This was a primary reason for their time in the wilderness—for God to reshape their worldview.

Above are two instances of worship, two expressions of play, with two different outcomes. They are both culturally expressive, but only one aligned with God's purposes and desires. This is the reason it is essential to use discernment when thinking about culture, including play. Otherwise, a theology of play can easily become culturally relativistic, embracing all forms of play, including ones that clearly oppose a biblical worldview. It is necessary to affirm cultural play that is innocent and pleasurable without judgment or dismissal. It is equally critical to challenge cultural play when it veers away from God's intentions. This requires a robust theologizing that applies wisdom to cultural play.

TRANSCULTURAL THEOLOGIZING

There are theological truths that transcend culture. This is true of the core beliefs of the Christian faith. The deity of Christ is not culture-bound. He is not the Savior of a culture but of all cultures (Rev. 7:9–11). Similarly, the nature of God cannot be interpreted differently depending on the culture. God stands outside of culture and speaks into it; he is not framed by it (Isa. 46:8–10). Equally, Scripture is not subject to cultural relativism; it transcends time (1 Peter 1:24–25).

However, there are certain aspects of the Christian faith that are shaped by culture. For example, how we interpret aspects of morality and community interactions is culturally informed. They are embedded within and expressed through a cultural framework. It is impossible to fully separate the two. For example, the Bible commands believers to pursue reconciliation when a conflict occurs (Matt. 5:23–24). For those in individualistic cultures, the onus is on the individuals and for the individuals. It oftentimes does not involve the community. For collectivistic cultures, it is not uncommon to include other members of the community, even a mediator at times.

Theologian Paul Hiebert developed a process to discern cultural beliefs and practices called *critical contextualization*. It involved four steps: exegesis of the culture, exegesis of Scripture, critical response, and new cultural practices (1984, 1987). While each culture has the right and responsibility to contextualize the Bible in their specific contexts, it is also necessary to engage with the global church (Hiebert 1985, 217). As Rochelle Cathcart and Mike Nichols stated, "It was out of this global dialogue that Hiebert envisioned the development of a biblically-based, supracultural, historical, christological, and Spirit-led 'transcultural theology' or 'metatheology' that would compare theologies, explore the cultural biases of each, and seek to find biblical universals" (2009, 212, referencing Hiebert 1985, 217–19). In other words, this theological bumping and dialogue chips away at the cultural trappings of a belief or practice toward a truer picture of God's intent and design.

To use conflict resolution as an example, by having the Western and Eastern approaches to reconciliation bump into one another, one can see more clearly God's foundational desire. The individualistic and collectivistic expressions inform yet also give way to an appreciation of the heart of reconciliation—to be at peace one to another, as individuals and community. Reconciliation elevates biblical unity and dependence upon the Holy Spirit. It is not about the individual or even the community but rather God's purposes and work among his people. Transcultural theologizing allows us to see the true essence of biblical commands and practices.

This process equally applies to play. To use the example of cultural dancing, it is good to have these expressions bump into one another. By doing so, we can discern the actual cultural practices and thus appreciate God's intent and desire of culturally expressed leisure and play. For example, one can compare the Adumu dance of the Maasai people of Kenya with modern nightclub dancing. Cultural expressions are embedded in both forms, collectivistic in the former and individualistic in the latter. They each produce happiness. They each encourage creativity. They each involve a group of people. The essence (or core) of both expressions is good. In this book, I have defined play as *the God-given ability and permission to fully enjoy moments in life as God intended, with freedom and pleasure.* As such, both forms of dancing produce enjoyment in life. They express freedom and pleasure. And their essence affirms and aligns with God's desire for people—to celebrate life. They reflect God's love for human enjoyment, and thus show us something of his nature. Yet, these cultural expressions of play can also fall out of line with God's purposes. If nightclub dancing begins to encourage lust by twerking or grinding, it becomes inappropriate. Or, if it results in violent behavior, such as when the Adumu dance is accompanied by the killing of a lion, it moves from being God's gift to a distortion. Or, in the case of the Israelites, dancing was an expression of idolatry.

Transcultural theologizing fosters discernment and wisdom. It clarifies and preserves God's original intent of play and thus allows the cultural expressions to be affirmed and celebrated while also safe-guarding against distortions that misalign God's purposes. It cultivates a Christian worldview that is neither ethnocentric nor ethno-controlling but God honoring. But, more so, it allows us to see more clearly the heart of God. It moves us past exotifying culture to seeing the Creator of all things, including play. In other words, it allows us to see the transcen-dent aspects of play that undergird and inform the cultural trappings of play. And this leads us to a celebration of play by acknowledging and affirming the Giver of it.

SOME KEY TAKEAWAYS

As we engage in transcultural theologizing, we can both celebrate and enjoy cultural play. This can move us beyond dismissing culture to celebrating it, from controlling it to enjoying it, which can enrich our lives and leisure.

We Should Enjoy Cultural Play

Cultural play is a gift from God. It uniquely expresses cultural values and traditions. It is not something that one should be ashamed of. It captures a person's cultural heritage and perspective. A person should have permission to celebrate it with richness and pride. Equally so, one should appreciate others' cultural play. By doing so, it can foster a celebration of God's unique gift of life to other cultures. It allows a person to step into perspective taking. It enables a person to embrace God's global world.

Recently, doctoral students from East Africa were in Lancaster for residency courses. It is rare for these students to see snow. I was thankful that one day a couple of inches fell on the ground. As we were leaving class, I stopped and knelt to the ground. I formed a snowball, then ran up behind my student from Congo. I gently threw the snowball at him and hit him on the chest. I turned around and invited all of them into a snowball fight. They quickly made snowballs and threw them back at me and at one another. We laughed and smiled. We played in the snow. It was the first time they had participated in a snowball fight. Even though a snowball fight is not explicitly cultural, it did not exist in their culture due to the absence of snow. And thus, in many respects, this was a cultural experience of play. As we piled into my van, I said, "You have now participated in an American snowball fight."

We Should Learn from Others' Cultural Play

Learning from other cultures enriches our own perspectives. It allows us to see life in a different way. This in turn cultivates depth and breadth of thinking and living. It is one thing to understand culture cognitively; it is another thing to learn from it. It can result in cross-cultural perspective taking, as well as expressing pleasure and enjoyment.

I encourage you to befriend a person from another culture. As you cultivate the relationship, ask them how they uniquely play in their culture. What do they find enjoyable about those experiences? How does their cultural play reflect their traditions and values? And what do they find different about your forms of play? This dialogue can teach you the cultural values and perspectives of someone who sees life differently than you. And, as you step away from those conversations, take time to thank God for the cultural kaleidoscope of play.

For me, I have not dialogued enough about cross-cultural play. I have asked my international friends about their cultural traditions and practices. I have listened to stories about child-rearing and marital customs. Yet the conversations rarely turn to play. I believe I am missing out on deep connections as a result. There is an authentic connection that can be forged when you talk about something that brings another person pleasure. It is personal and honoring.

We Should Play in Others' Cultural Play

Play is a universal phenomenon and thus can be shared by everyone. Cultural play affords us the unique opportunity to be immersed, even for a moment, in someone else's world. It is in many respects a safe and vulnerable way to relationally connect with another person. When you are new to a game, no one expects you to have mastered it. Thus, you can be silly and clumsy. And, surprisingly enough, you might learn how to play more fully and naturally. It might allow you to rediscover the freedom and pleasure of play because there is no pressure or pretense.

My wife and I lived in London, England, for over a year. We were serving on staff in an evangelical Anglican church. It was a rich time of ministry engagement and development. One of the unique experiences during our time there was the church's quiz night. In the United States, quiz nights do not exist. If they do, we had never heard of any. In essence, you created a team, typically of four to six people. On the evening of the event, everyone showed up at church. We got situated at our designated table with snacks and some wine. There was an MC for the evening. After some introductions, this person then proceeded to ask obscure trivia questions. They involved history, literature, and sports. Each group worked together to address the questions. When the team had an answer, a member of that group raised a hand and shared what it was. If correct, that team received a point. The evening concluded when a group was declared the winner, after successfully answering the most questions. I like to believe I am intelligent. I want to think I know a great deal about history, literature, and sports. But this evening was a humbling experience, as I tried to answer a question about an event that occurred in 1283 in British history, two centuries before Christopher Columbus set foot in America. Or, when a short, obscure verse from a Shakespearean work was recited, I had difficulty identifying the play. In that moment, I looked blankly at my team and said, "I got nothing." And while I know American football, I was clearly not up to speed on my cricket history.

I failed miserably that evening. I may have gotten a couple of answers correct. Thankfully, one of the members of our team was an archivist, so we did quite well. But I had a blast. It was an enjoyable memory. I was not concerned about getting answers correct. It produced no embarrassment or frustration. I knew I was not going to do well because I am not British. And, since I had never participated in a quiz night, there were no expectations. Well, perhaps there were some expectations that I would do poorly. If so, I met them. As such, I relaxed. I enjoyed myself. And I played with freedom and pleasure.

SUMMARIZING THOUGHTS

A joyful heart is good medicine,
  but a crushed spirit dries up the bones. (Prov. 17:22)

Playfulness is good for our souls. It is medicinal. As our world becomes more globalized, we should enjoy the diversity of cultural play. It not only enriches our understanding of others but also enhances our view of God. It can capture a broader imagination of our Creator and can allow us to celebrate the unique difference in others. And it can soften our own stodginess. Cultural play is a gift. We should enjoy these gifts.

REFLECTION

I encourage you to step outside of your cultural group and engage the world. It is a beautiful place, reflecting God's unique and varied creativity. We are made in the image of God, with unique personalities, physical features, and cultural practices. It is healthy to interact with the global community. It can lighten us. It can refresh us. And it can stimulate us toward broader expressions of play.

1. Reflect on your own cultural play. What does this play communicate about your values, traditions, and perspectives?

2. Explore the cultural play of others. What might this play communicate about their values, traditions, and perspectives?

3. Engage in some cross-cultural dialogue, particularly around play. Ask others questions about their leisure practices.

4. Participate in another culture's play. If you know someone from another culture, ask them to introduce you to their experiences and expressions of play. If you do not know someone from another culture, go online and research forms of play and give them a go. Or, better yet, get to know someone from another culture and begin discovering their culture.

5. Reflect on God's gift of play to a diverse world. What does cultural play say about God's nature and character? What does this say about God's desires for us?

CHAPTER 7

Learning to Forgive: Playing Involves Removing Unnecessary Baggage

One cannot satisfy thirst by drinking seawater.
    —Galadriel, *The Lord of the Rings: The Rings of Power*

Life can be cruel. I sometimes imagine that we are on a journey in life. We are born without any concerns or burdens. In essence, we start with an empty backpack. The future is bright with anticipation and hope. As we grow older, we experience hurt—a mean comment or bullying experience. With each pain, we put a rock into this backpack. Sometimes this rock is a pebble; other times it is a small stone. Adolescence can be especially difficult, and sometimes we find our backpack getting full. It leads to a bit of cynicism, as life doesn't appear as good as it once did. Adulthood presents its own hardships of broken relationships and coworker betrayals. At times, the rocks we add to our backpack are a result of an organization or, sadly, the church, letting us down. With this increasing weight, we find ourselves slumped over with our eyes downcast and legs buckling. Life is no longer good but cruel. It is possible by the time we reach middle age that our hands and knees are calloused from the times we had to crawl simply to move forward. The pain from divorce or cancer becomes too much to bear at times. There is no longer any joy in life.

This is a depressing way to begin this chapter. I know. You might be thinking, "I am going to skip to chapter 7 and go where we can talk more about play and this enjoying life stuff." I encourage you to put aside that pull and sit in this chapter. The reason is that I believe this imagery characterizes many in this world. Hurts pile up, and with each pain, life becomes harder and harder. Yes, we compartmentalize life by rationalizing the jabs and the betrayals, sometimes believing the next phase of life will be better. If I can only survive high school, I will be OK. Other times we try to tilt the scale the other way by adding excitement to our life, hoping this will counterbalance the scars. For some, this involves chasing experiences. Others might pursue relationships with the hope that something or someone new will erase the previous pains. None of these options are effective. It is tantamount to ignoring the backpack while holding hands with someone. It might distract us for a moment, but it doesn't eliminate the hurt.

This backpack filled with stones and rocks directly impacts our ability to play. It is impossible to consistently enjoy life with pleasure and freedom if we are becoming increasingly crushed under the weight of pain and hurt. To truly play, we must remove the unnecessary and unwanted baggage in our lives. In this chapter, I want to walk us through how hurt truly impacts us. This will most certainly be uncomfortable at times. Yet I do not want to leave us in the mire of pain but move us toward hope and freedom through the embrace of forgiveness. As much as we try not to let it, pain has a direct influence on our view of God. Wrestling with life's cruelty from the safety of God's forgiveness can enable us, stone by stone, to heal the damaging wounds accumulated over the years. And from this healing can emerge a newfound discovery of enjoyment and play.

THE EFFECTS OF HURT

Hurt can take many forms and mar us in numerous ways. One study explored the impact of social rejection, concluding that it negatively influenced self-esteem and self-worth, whereas individuals who were accepted experienced "happy feelings" (Blackhart et al. 2009, 294). Another study detailed how childhood maltreatment is associated with "violent behavior, mood disorders, and non-suicidal and suicidal self-injury" (Liu 2019,

221). I don't believe this research is surprising to anyone. It is intuitive that hurt can deeply shape us negatively.

Hurt Mars Us Emotionally

Significant trauma shapes us for years, if not decades. For example, individuals who faced domestic violence in childhood experience emotional fractures well into adulthood that impact relationships, employment, and mental health (Hague 2012). These large stones negatively shape us. They suffocate us. Negative emotions linger and shape our perspectives. They cultivate in us a suspicion toward the world, particularly relationships. If unresolved, they make us cautious and guarded, as a defensive mechanism to avoid hurt again. In contrast, positive emotions increase social connections and mental wellness (Gruber and Moskowitz 2014). They encourage freedom and enjoyment. They can lead to happiness.

We can each remember those childhood or adolescent memories of being rejected or ridiculed. They are seared in our minds. It might be difficult to remember a conversation we had two months ago with a friend, but we have a photographic memory when it comes to pain. And if the pain is amplified to the traumatic level, we not only remember it but still feel it. Addressing these hurts will move us toward freedom and thus enjoyment of life.

Hurt Mars Us Relationally

Unless there is trauma, children naturally trust other people. For them, there is an innocence to life. Life would be utopian if this remained true into adulthood. We would then be able to enjoy social interactions and relationships without the pain of judgment, abuse, or rejection. Sadly, this is not the case. Very quickly we experience the full weight of the Fall. And, as the relational hurts continue to occur, it can feel like death by a thousand paper cuts.

Sin has a devastating effect on relationships. The Bible is filled with stories of how sin destroyed families and friends (Gen. 4:1–12; 2 Sam. 13:1–22; 1 Cor. 6:1–8). Relational hurt also victimizes us twice over. It not only impacts the original relationship where the hurt occurred but also influences future relationships. A daughter who was hurt by a father will typically have a guarded view toward other males; they are seen as untrustworthy. If a girlfriend cheated on you, you then view future relationships suspiciously. A coworker who betrayed your confidence will cause you to think, "Hurt me once, shame on you; hurt me twice, shame on me." This hurt causes us to enter relationships with an automatic deficit because we believe people are not always safe. Rather than viewing the best in another person and thus being able to fully enjoy that relationship, we approach them with emotional armor.

Hurt Mars Us Spiritually

We are interconnected individuals. Relationships impact our emotions, and emotions impact our souls. When we are hurt in life, it can spill over to our relationships with God and other Christians. During my years as a pastor, I met numerous individuals who rejected God because of a pain they experienced in life. In fact, oftentimes the people most adamantly against Christianity were the ones who lost a loved one in a car accident or due to cancer. They believe that God hurt them; therefore, they rejected God. In some ways, it is a sort of revenge—"God, you hurt me. I will now hurt you by rejecting you."

In a similar fashion, I found that the individuals who most resisted the church were the ones who had been hurt by believers. Perhaps it was legalism that caused guilt. In some cases, it was a dictatorial leader who weaponized the Bible to make people feel shame. I remember a member of my congregation who experienced public ridicule in her childhood church. If you disobeyed any of the church stances on behavior, they would bring you up to the front of the church on Sunday, publicly announce your "sin," and proceed to shame you. She eventually found her way to our church. By this time, she was in her late forties, married, with a teenage son. These childhood events continued to cause her to need psychological treatment and therapy. It had an erosive effect on church relationships ("I am not sure anyone is safe") and her family ("I am a horrible wife and mother"). At times, she would say, "Everyone would be better off without me." She had difficulty trusting God because she questioned why God would allow her past hurt. And, for obvious reasons, she found it very challenging to trust another believer, let alone a leader in the church.

HOW DOES HURT RELATE TO PLAY?

Experiencing a moment of hurt can be brushed off as a singular event. The accumulation of hurts over the years, however, erodes our perspective. Worse yet, a traumatic event such as abuse or infidelity deeply damages our psyche and soul. Over time, hurts cause us to see the world as unsafe and cruel rather than safe and good. And when we live with the presumption that life is unsafe and cruel, we will likely find it difficult to truly enjoy life.

It is possible to play with backpacks of rocks on our backs. A person can enjoy friends, activities, and experiences. Yet I would argue that it is difficult to consistently play with true freedom and pleasure because either we are hanging onto the hurt or the hurt resounds in our subconscious, preventing us from truly playing. The whispers to be cautious, be guarded, and tread lightly echo in our ears. In chapter 5, I discussed play as being therapeutic. This applies to momentary bad days. Play can be a remedy for these singular events. The backpack full of hurt requires a different response. It necessitates a restoration, a redemption of our view of life from it being cruel to it being safe again.

Safety is necessary to truly play. It allows us to step into relationships and experiences without tentativeness. It enables us to be our true selves in these moments. It even allows us to embrace risk by playing without concern for others' opinions. It cultivates freedom and pleasure. To do so requires us to see God as for us and others as not against us. And in time, our perspective of the world can gradually change toward one that is good.

My wife and I strive to cultivate a home that is safe. We want our children to feel completely accepted and secure. It is our desire that they can *truly be* when they are at home—a place where we can be our true selves around each other. One of our great joys as parents is that our children love to spend time with each other. They affectionately refer to each other as "best friends," even at twenty-two and eighteen. At times, we will hear them talking on the phone, laughing and teasing each other. When they are home, they love to play together by grabbing a bite to eat, watching a movie, or playing *Beat Saber* on the VR headset. They have the unique ability to make the other person laugh at any moment. They know *how* to play together, and they love playing *with* each other. Obviously, this ability has been cultivated through a friendship of shared experiences and mutual support. Yet, more so, it was birthed out of the safety they feel with one another. Because they feel safe, they can be themselves with one another without pretense or caution. This is the power of play when we feel safe.

FORGIVENESS CULTIVATES SAFETY

Forgiveness frees us from the hurt. It does not erase the memory of the pain; however, it does remove the sting of that pain. Ephesians 4:31–32 states, "Let all bitterness and wrath and anger and clamor and slander be put away from you, along with all malice. Be kind to one another, tender-hearted, forgiving one another, as God in Christ forgave you." Paul was describing the relationship between "bitterness, wrath, and anger" and forgiveness. By forgiving others, the unhealthy emotions are removed or "put away." There is freedom in forgiveness.

There are specific objects of forgiveness. At times, we need to forgive others. There are also times when we need to forgive an organization. While there are people behind those institutions, it can be difficult to identify the person responsible for the hurt, thus the necessity to forgive the agency of that hurt. There is also a need to forgive ourselves.

Forgiveness of Others

People hurt us. It is a reality of the human experience in a world involving sinful persons. Inevitably, we will hurt others, and we will be hurt. At times, this is inadvertent; other times it is intentional. If it is intentional, it highlights a deeper problem needing to be addressed. Yet inadvertent hurts also require forgiveness. They still sting. It is not helpful to simply dismiss the hurt by saying, "The person didn't mean it. No worries." This can lead to a guardedness over time if it continues. But it also isn't helpful to confront individuals every time there is an inadvertent hurt. Sometimes it is necessary to forgive without a conversation. On the other hand, if it is intentional, it is necessary to challenge the behavior; otherwise, the sin goes unaddressed, and the behavior might continue, either to you or to someone else.

The story of Joseph and his brothers is a raw account of the internal tension between revenge and forgiveness. We see Joseph moving back and forth between the two throughout the narrative. When Joseph first saw his brothers in Egypt, he was angry and began to plot revenge (Gen. 42:6–17). During this first encounter, in the same moment, he bound Simeon as collateral to ensure his brothers' return to Egypt (movement toward revenge), and he also wept (movement toward forgiveness) (Gen. 42:24). There was a conflict over whether to forgive or to seek revenge. When they returned a second time, he invited them to dinner (Gen. 43; movement toward forgiveness), but then he filled their sacks with grain, returned their money, and placed his cup in Benjamin's sack to entrap them (Gen. 44; movement toward revenge). He then demanded the imprisonment of Benjamin (Gen. 44:17; movement toward revenge) before finally weeping and revealing himself to his brothers (Gen. 45:1–4; arrival at forgiveness). During this wrestling, the key to his forgiveness was seeing God's providence at work. He stated in verse 5, "And now do not be distressed or angry with yourselves because you sold me here, for God sent me before you to preserve life." True forgiveness required God working in the midst of the pain. True forgiveness is never an act of the human will; it involves God's grace, power, and perspective.

Malachy McCourt stated, "Resentment is like taking poison and waiting for the other person to die" (quoted in Witchel 1998). This vivid statement captures the destructive nature of resentment—it harms the other person in that reconciliation is never attempted, and it erodes oneself through the ravaging power of bitterness. It is obvious that a resentful person is not able to enjoy life; they are concerned with inflicting pain. This mindset stifles freedom and pleasure; it enslaves rather than gives life. These are not the conditions for play. It is necessary to move toward forgiveness until we arrive at it if we are to fully enjoy life.

Forgiveness of Organizations

Organizational hurt can take many forms. It can involve an abusive church, as described above. It can be a business or institution that devalues employee worth. It can be the government who treats its citizens unfairly.

Yes, organizations are comprised of people; thus, ultimately it is people who hurt. However, organizations take on a culture. And sometimes this culture can inflict pain.

If you have been hurt by an organization, it is necessary to release it. In Luke 23:34, while on the cross, Jesus stated, "Father, forgive them, for they know not what they do." The human objects of this forgiveness are the individuals who crucified him—the guards. Yet, I believe Jesus was referring not only to the guards but to the system. The guards were carrying out the orders decreed to them by the Roman Empire. They were products of a system that devalued life and indiscriminately executed people. In essence, they were doing their jobs as part of a sinful system—everyone from Pilate to Herod to the guards. Jesus was asking for forgiveness of the system that propagated such conduct.

I know several friends who have experienced institutional racism. They have been treated unjustly. They have been demeaned through verbal attacks. And sometimes their pain has been dismissed when a superficial offer of Christian forgiveness was given without attempting to understand the true weight of the hurt. In these cases, it is essential for the victims to challenge the system. It is critical to seek change. Yet, it is biblically necessary to also forgive. Without forgiveness, it will be impossible to cultivate emotional freedom—an essential ingredient to play.

A Personal Appeal

Before I move to the final arena of forgiveness, I want to personally appeal to those that have been deeply traumatized and victimized by hurt. There are pains that are hard to fathom. The evil that a person can inflict on another person makes my stomach turn and crushes my spirit. I cannot understand this pain; very few can. Jesus fully understands this pain. He was innocent yet beaten and crucified, *and* he was able to forgive. I believe the crucifixion, and all the horror unleashed on our perfect Savior, provides the foundation and the ability for any person, even those who have faced the worst of humanity, to forgive. It provides light in the dark places. It offers freedom out of the prison. It enables hope in the midst of hopelessness. God does not want you to be shackled in pain. He wants you to experience true freedom and enjoyment. He died so that you could be free—free from the pain and free from the shame. God deeply longs for you to enjoy life again *in true freedom and pleasure*!

Forgiveness of Self

My wife and I love the movie *The Mission*. It is a fictitious but historically accurate film depicting the accounts of a Jesuit missionary in eighteenth-century South America. It unpacks colonialism. It depicts contextualization. It details how these missionaries attempted to protect an indigenous village from destruction by members of pro-slavery Portugal. One of the lead characters is Rodrigo Mendoza, a mercenary and slave trader. In the movie, his wife commits infidelity. In a fit of rage, he kills her lover. Overcome with remorse, he descends into depression. Father Gabriel, a Jesuit priest, approaches him with an offer of penance. Rodrigo accepts this offer and proceeds to carry a heavy bag filled with armor and swords for miles through rugged terrain. One powerful scene is of him carrying it up a large waterfall. He struggles to grab ahold of each rock crevice during the climb while being pulled down by the weight of the bag. When he eventually reaches the village (the place he terrorized with his slave trading) he collapses in exhaustion and repentance. One of the village boys comes over to him and cuts the bag free. It crashes over the side of a river ledge. Symbolically, the bag represents the burden of his sin. Throughout the journey, he was not able to forgive himself until the moment this villager cuts the bag free. I do not support penance. However, this scene depicts the necessity of forgiving oneself.

Sometimes we are the ones who are not hurt but the ones who do the hurting. The only appropriate response is to repent and seek forgiveness. Depending on the nature of the hurt, it very well might require forgiveness of self. 1 John 1:9 states, "If we confess our sins, he is faithful and just to forgive us our sins and to cleanse us from all unrighteousness." God will forgive our sins—not just certain sins, but all sins. If this is true, it is quite audacious to be unwilling to forgive ourselves when a perfect God is willing to do so. It might require deep soul-searching and personal confession. However, in the end, it is essential to move toward forgiveness. We need to forgive ourselves because punishing ourselves (a form of emotional penance) prevents us from experiencing true freedom.

GOD IS SAFE

True forgiveness requires the affirmation and belief that God is safe. This is paramount. Only God can help us truly forgive. It is one of the unique truths of the Christian faith. The passages that detail forgiveness always link our need to forgive others as a response to God's forgiveness of us—"forgiving each other; as the Lord has forgiven you, so you also must forgive" (Col. 3:13; see also Eph. 4:32). God delights in forgiveness. He delights when we offer forgiveness. And he creates a safe arena for us to move toward forgiveness—in time and amid all the emotions that offenses create.

God's safety is not cuddly. It is rooted in his sovereignty, power, and goodness (Isa. 46:8–10; Rev. 7:12; Ps. 107:1). God's sovereignty ensures that the necessary issues and emotions are addressed. He sees what is in a person (1 Sam. 16:7) and thus can pull out the anger and resentment, even the deep emotions that have been calloused over. God's power permits and ensures true forgiveness. One does not have to wonder if forgiveness occurred if it is done through and in God's power. It enables a genuine movement of the heart. God's goodness invites the person to honestly wrestle through the emotions of an offense and release the bitterness and resentment. It allows us to see freedom as better than bondage. Goodness enables us to be present in the pain as we move toward forgiveness. It is an expression of God's tenderness and grace to us.

God is described as *Abba Father* (Rom. 8:15). This father is sovereign, powerful, and good. He is a father without discrimination or capriciousness. He is fair, just, and loving. He desires our hearts to be restored and our relationships to be reconciled. He is the one who is most for us. He longs for our healing and delights in our forgiveness. And he desires deeply for us to experience his attribute of forgiveness—to self and to others. This is the safety of God. From this safety we can receive forgiveness. From this safety we can extend forgiveness.

FORGIVENESS AND CELEBRATION

The parable of the prodigal son is a powerful example of forgiveness and celebration (Luke 15:11–32). The story recounts a man who had two sons. The younger son demanded his inheritance prior to his father's passing. This boldness would be culturally offensive, in essence communicating to the father, "I wish you were already dead." The father granted the son's wish. The father would have experienced deep shame. His son disrespected him. It is likely he would have been mocked by the community. The normal response would be for the son to be immediately disinherited, not given the inheritance.

The son traveled to a distant land and squandered the inheritance, eventually finding employment at a pig farm. There is no indication in the story as to the amount of time that had passed. But I imagine anger, disappointment, guilt, and grief arising many times in the father when the son left and during his time away. This would be a normal human response. Depressed by his situation, the son decided to return to his father in the hopes that he could gain better employment as a servant.

> While [the son] was still a long way off, his father saw him and felt compassion, and ran and embraced him and kissed him. And the son said to him, "Father, I have sinned against heaven and before you. I am no longer worthy to be called your son." But the father said to his servants, "Bring quickly the best robe, and put it on him, and put a ring on his hand, and shoes on his feet." (Luke 15:20–24)

The father had compassion, thus forgiveness, even prior to the son's repentance. The father had been *moving toward forgiveness already*. The son's repentance was directed toward God ("against heaven") and his father ("before you"), affirming that *he was inviting God into his remorse*. True repentance and forgiveness require the working of God. It seems likely that the son had forgiven himself, displayed by his willing return to the father and acceptance of his father's compassion and restoration of his status (v. 22).

The forgiveness then leads to a party. The father says, "'And bring the fattened calf and kill it, and let us eat and *celebrate*. For this my son was dead, and is alive again; he was lost, and is found.' And they began to *celebrate*" (vv. 23–24). The father holds a party for the family, workers, and community. He is celebrating his son's return. And, more foundationally, he is celebrating the *power of forgiveness that leads to restoration.*

Forgiveness created the conditions for play—the celebration. The father was able to celebrate because his resentment had been removed through forgiveness. It would have been impossible to play if he maintained his bitterness. Even if he threw a party, he would have been emotionally detached because of his anger. Forgiveness enabled him to fully enjoy this moment with pleasure. The younger son was able to play because he had forgiven himself and received the father's forgiveness. If he had remained in his guilt, he would have been unable to participate in the celebration. Granting himself forgiveness and receiving his father's forgiveness allowed him to be fully present in this moment, celebrating forgiveness and restoration. The community partook in this event because the father's willingness and ability to forgive enabled the community to celebrate. Forgiveness gives permission for others to play. And most importantly, God celebrates as the one who gives the power to forgive. God fully enjoys the moments his people play, particularly in response to forgiveness and reconciliation.

Sadly, there is one person who is not able to play in this event—the older son. "Now his older son was in the field, and as he came and drew near to the house, he heard *music and dancing*" (v. 25). The older son hears the party—music, dancing, food, and celebration. Everyone was playing except him! But the older son "was *angry* and *refused* to go in" (v. 28). When his father approaches him, he states, "Look, these many years I have served you, and I never disobeyed your command, yet you never gave me a young goat, that I might celebrate with my friends. But when this son of yours came, who has devoured your property with prostitutes, you killed the fattened calf for him!" (vv. 29–30). He even referred to his brother as "this son of yours," amplifying his deep anger. The son *had not moved toward forgiveness* but remained in his resentment. As a result, he was not willing to participate in the party—"he refused to go in." He was not able to play because he continued to be engulfed in his bitterness. The lack of forgiveness prevented him from celebrating life, from playing.

Forgiveness cultivates safety that allows individuals to fully enjoy life with freedom and pleasure. It grants the gift of freedom and pleasure within oneself by freeing the self from shame and guilt. It grants the gift of freedom and pleasure to the one offended by releasing the bitterness and resentment. It grants the gift of freedom and pleasure to others by elevating relationship and community. And this allows us and others to truly play, free from the shackles of hurt and pain.

SUMMARIZING THOUGHTS

There is a relationship between forgiveness and play. If we are harboring anger and bitterness from hurt, either large or small, it is impossible to consistently enjoy life with freedom and pleasure. Hurt suffocates our joy and happiness. Thus, a prerequisite to true play involves dealing with the unnecessary baggage in our lives—the hurts accumulated over the years. It consists of taking each stone, rock, and boulder, and processing it, reflecting upon it, and eventually removing it by embracing forgiveness through the power of Christ.

REFLECTION

As you reflect on this chapter, think about your baggage. What hurts do you need to work on as you move toward forgiveness? How is your enjoyment in life being suffocated by these hurts?

1. Take some time in the upcoming weeks to write down the unresolved hurts in your life. Begin to pray about how God can work to remove those stones and rocks.

2. Invite God's spirit into this process. Ask him to help you with all the emotions, guardedness, and hesitations preventing you from moving toward forgiveness.

3. Spend some time reflecting on the parable of the prodigal son. Who do you most resonate with in this story?

4. Imagine the freedom and pleasure that is possible on the other side of forgiveness. What might this look like in your life?

5. When you do forgive, go celebrate God's work in your life. Go play as an expression of God's sovereignty, power, and goodness displayed through forgiveness.

CHAPTER 8

Learning to Live in Freedom: Playing Involves Putting Aside Guilt and Shame

Christian freedom does not mean being free to do as we like; it means being free to do as we ought.
—William Barclay

Our house was a gathering place for our children's friends while our children were in high school. It was not uncommon for a group of kids to come over on the weekends, play basketball, and enjoy a bonfire. There was no alcohol or questionable behavior. It was clean, good fun. At times, we asked our daughter if it was "cool" to have everyone to our house, especially as a senior. She typically responded, "I love it. It is nice to have a house where everyone can hang out and have fun. It is much better than going to a party and getting drunk. Why would you want to do that? You lose your senses, you don't remember the party, and you feel awful the next day. I would much rather enjoy volleyball and s'mores in our back yard."

I am very thankful our kids had this perspective. I recognize it is not common. In many cases in our world today, a party is only fun if it involves alcohol and people hooking up. In essence, a good time is tossing morals aside and partying without inhibition. Play here involves *freedom to do whatever we want without moral constraints.* It is freedom to let go and let loose.

In this chapter we are going to talk about how freedom relates to play. We will discover that freedom is viewed in radically different ways depending on your worldview, and this shapes our understanding of play. To fully understand freedom, it is important to first unpack the notions of guilt and shame.

GUILT AND SHAME

Guilt

Guilt is oftentimes resisted. It is commonly viewed as a bad thing. When someone communicates a moral standard to another person, a typical response is, "Don't make me feel guilty. That might be true for you, but it is not true for me." This is humanism influencing our perspective. Guilt does not feel good; therefore, it cannot be good. This opens the door for moral relativism.

Leroy Aden and David Brenner stated that guilt is failure in light of someone else's expectation whereas shame is failure in light of our own ideal (1989). From a Christian perspective, guilt involves our relationship with God and the standards he has set before us. It is judicial in nature. It is grounded in God's attributes—holiness and purity. It is God's mechanism to convict us of moral failure. In this sense, guilt is good.

Scripture views guilt as good and beneficial. In Genesis 3, Adam and Eve felt guilt when they violated God's commands. Guilt is intended to prompt repentance and restoration. Guilt is experienced in the context of worship when people approach God without reverence (Exod. 28:38, 43; Lev. 22:16). It is also connected to violating community when individuals sin against another person (Lev. 5:16–19; 10:17; 19:17). Moses asked Aaron's sons, "Why didn't you eat the sin offering in the sanctuary area? It is most holy; it was given to you to take away the guilt of the *community* by making atonement for them before the LORD" (Lev. 10:17 NIV).

Leviticus 4:2–3 states, "If anyone sins *unintentionally* in any of the LORD's commandments about things not to be done, and does any one of them, if it is the anointed priest who sins, thus bringing guilt on the people, then he shall offer for the sin that he has committed a bull from the herd without blemish to the LORD for a sin offering." In this passage, unintentional sin also produces guilt because the sin is a violation of God's transcendent law. It is not dependent on our motivation, knowledge, or agreement. Prior to accepting Christ, I oftentimes experienced guilt over moral lapses even though I did not affirm biblical truth. This was because I was violating God's moral standards, which were applicable to me even as a non-Christian. Unfortunately, as was true for me, it is possible to harden one's heart to the promptings of guilt and thus continue to engage in immoral behavior.

Guilt is fundamentally a breach in relationship. Baker's *Evangelical Dictionary of Biblical Theology* states,

> The Hebrew noun *asham* [אָשָׁם] means both "guilt" (e.g., Jer. 51:5) and "guilt offering" (the term used in Lev. 5:14–19; 7:1–10, etc.). The difference between "guilt" and "sin" is important here. Whereas the words for "sin" focus on its quality as an act or as personal failure, *asham* [אָשָׁם] points to the *breach in relationships that sin causes*, and in particular to the indebtedness that results. (Elwell 1996, 319; emphasis mine)

More broadly, guilt highlights our broken relationship with God. Sin is imputed to us because of Adam's sin (Rom. 5:12). Thus, we have been found guilty. Because of this imputed sin, we live under the state of guilt. To remove this state of guilt, it is necessary to receive the imputation of Christ's righteousness (2 Cor. 5:21). This ultimately removes the guilt by restoring our relationship with God. It doesn't eliminate guilt from sinful actions, but it does eradicate the core guilt due to our fallen nature.

Shame

Shame, on the other hand, relates to one's *personhood*. It impacts how we see ourselves before God and others. According to Baker,

> Shame is a consequence of sin. . . . Though related to guilt, shame emphasizes sin's effect on *self-identity*. . . . The first response of Adam and Eve to their sinful condition was to hide from God, and consequently from one another (Gen. 3:7–8; 2:25). (Elwell 1996, 734–35, emphasis mine)

There was shame in how they viewed themselves. Shame captures the idea of "self-failure." There is a sense of defeat and despair within oneself. With shame, there is a perception that we need to hide, consciously or subconsciously, physically or emotionally. It prompts embarrassment. It can lead to rage toward another person. And, more damaging, it distorts our identity. The Bible affirms that people embroiled in sin experience shame (Phil. 3:19) but also that God can remove one's shame (Isa. 45:17; 61:7). When one accepts Christ, shame is removed (Rom. 9:33; 10:11; 1 Peter 2:6; Heb. 12:2).

To summarize, guilt is an awareness of failure against a *standard*. Shame is a sense of failure before *the eyes of someone*. Guilt is more volitional; shame is more emotive. Guilt is based on a transcendent law; shame is based on self-perception. Guilt is atoned for in Christ; shame drives us to the atonement.

False Guilt

False guilt involves *perceived failure* that is not biblically supported. It is the notion that we have violated God's standards when in fact we have not. An example in Scripture is eating food sacrificed to idols (1 Cor. 8:7–8). Paul stated that there is nothing wrong with eating food offered in such a manner. It is simply food. However, he stated that some people feel guilty for doing so. He referred to them as having "weak" consciences. In other words, they have false guilt based on a perceived moral failure that is not upheld in Scripture.

False guilt typically revolves around behavior. I had a glass of wine and thus feel guilty because someone stated (in my specific Christian community or from my childhood) that good Christians do not drink. I listened to secular music, watched a particular movie, or even read a dystopian novel involving sorcery and thus feel guilty. False guilt can lead to confusion in that the person does not understand why something is wrong. Granted, it is important to be wise. Christians should embrace things that uplift our soul, not malign it. Further, we should avoid behavior if it might cause someone else to struggle, such as drinking alcohol in the presence of an alcoholic. Yet, at its core, we should not attach Christian maturity to behaviors that are viewed as morally neutral in Scripture.

HOW DOES GUILT AND SHAME CONNECT TO PLAY?

We have discussed various types of play throughout this book. Play involves sports, concerts, hobbies, and spontaneous moments of enjoyment, such as dancing in a field. These playful expressions are oftentimes innocent, thus not producing guilt or shame. A person should feel no guilt for going to a football game. Shame should not be experienced from sailing. Yet play oftentimes crosses the line morally. Increasingly in our society, liberating play necessitates defying moral boundaries. Therefore, it is essential to unpack how we should view freedom as it relates to play. Are there limits to playful expression? And, if so, how do we discern those limits?

Freedom in the Eyes of Society

Freedom in society is becoming more and more equated with no restraints, no limits, and even no moral compass. There are very few moral guardrails. This connects deeply to play. As Katharine Hebhurn stated, "If you obey all the rules, you miss all the fun" (Crimp 2003, 30). There is a sentiment in today's culture that having fun means immoral conduct. Play involves freedom to do whatever I want in the manner I want. There are no moral constraints. You can play however you want, regardless of whether it is immoral. To play in this manner is intentionally ignoring God's moral purposes and thus squelching shame and guilt. If guilt is violating a moral standard and shame is acknowledgment of self-failure to that standard, the easiest remedy to guilt and shame is to discard the standard. The absence of moral standards allows a person to "be free" to play however they want. As stated, this perspective is a natural by-product of humanism—life is for self and for one's own pleasure. No one should tell me how I can have fun, especially not God.

I would argue that play in the eyes of the world is oftentimes an escape and not true enjoyment. Certainly, it can produce a moment of pleasure and happiness. Yet play expressed outside of God's moral standard eventually leads to internal despair and relational brokenness. For example, sexual play experienced outside of God's standard leads to emptiness and depression. It further leads to diminished esteem by degrading relationships rather than upholding them. It even has future consequences by tainting intimate experiences by reducing sexual experiences to pleasure only. Similarly, to the observer, getting drunk can be perceived as fun and thus an expression of play by promoting freedom from seriousness, work, and responsibility. At the end of a difficult week or after a breakup, society encourages play through getting smashed or hooking up with someone. Yet one must ask if this is true freedom. Are you truly free if the next morning you are filled with guilt and shame? Are you truly free if relationships are tarnished or your identity is scarred? Should not freedom lift you up rather than hollow you?

Freedom in the Eyes of God

Freedom in Christ involves living within God's moral standards. It recognizes that play is designed to be enjoyed and expressed within the guardrails of moral precepts. It affirms that humans are created in God's image and thus nurtured and built up by embracing play that is life-giving.

Galatians 5:1 states, "For freedom Christ has set us free; stand firm therefore, and do not submit again to a yoke of slavery." This passage affirms the freedom available through a relationship with Jesus, in contrast to one that is bound by the law. In Romans 8:2, when discussing the Holy Spirit, Paul wrote, "For the law of the Spirit of life has set you free in Christ Jesus from the law of sin and death." In Christ, we are no longer bound to the guilt and shame that plagues humanity. We enjoy freedom from the guilt incurred through Adam, and we no longer need to experience shame since we are called children of God (1 John 3:1–2). Our identity is in Christ.

Playing as Christians means we enjoy life fully by living within God's moral purposes. This requires being sensitive to guilt—those divine convictions when we veer outside the moral guardrails—and striving to cultivate a deep self-identity in Christ that repels shame. Granted, we are not perfect; therefore, there will always be struggles with guilt and shame, including false guilt that whispers for us to abstain from perceived sinful behavior. Playing within a biblical framework allows us to be fully and truly free to enjoy life's pleasures. We can be free to play because we do not have to conform to the world's understanding of play—one that throws off moral constraints and strives to live without boundaries. We can be free to play because we will not face the guilt and shame that accompanies worldly play.

Play is defined as *the God-given ability and permission to fully enjoy moments in life as God intended, with freedom and pleasure.* Within this definition, the focus is on "as God intended." This has a dual meaning. God desires for us to play. Yet also the manner of that play is not up to the individual; it is framed around God's moral desires and attributes. It is the manner of play that God intends for us. True play occurs within God's moral parameters. This form of play is superior to the worldly form of play, in that it offers genuine freedom and pleasure without guilt and shame.

I lived outside of God's moral constraints in high school prior to coming to Christ. I would party on the weekends, which sometimes consisted of getting drunk. I had a fake ID; therefore, I was able to purchase alcohol whenever I wanted to. For me and my friends, fun became associated with drinking beer. Usually, it was cheap beer since this was all we could afford. It almost became the standard that one was not truly having fun if they were not inebriated. Play equaled drinking a lot, losing one's senses, and waking up with a hangover the next day. Thankfully, this period in my life predated social media, so there isn't visual record of it. In the moment, in that season, I believed I was exercising my freedom—over my body and in defiance of the law. I believed this was true pleasure.

During this same season, a growing emptiness was stirring in my life. I found partying to be dissatisfying. Drinking excessively did not produce fulfillment. Relationships seemed shallow. I could not shake the guilt and shame, and these feelings eventually led me to Christ.

Contrast this experience with my daughter's twenty-first birthday. As one of her gifts, my wife and I took her to an open-air restaurant and bar in Lancaster called The Exchange. It has an incredible vibe. There are fire torches at each table. It overlooks the city. Inside, you can recline on couches while enjoying a drink. We chose the outside area so we could watch the sunset. We each ordered a drink to celebrate this milestone in our daughter's life. We laughed. We reminisced. We celebrated. Our relationships were deepened. And a memory was created that we will cherish for years.

Let's compare these two events. They both involved alcohol. They both revolved around relationships. And laughter and fun were present in both situations. Yet, it was the latter that produced true freedom and pleasure, and honestly the more vivid memory. There was no guilt or shame with my wife and daughter. I did not feel empty or hollow. I was enjoying a drink with my family to celebrate my daughter turning twenty-one. I believe God took delight in this moment because we were playing together within his moral constraints.

AN EXAMPLE: SEXUAL PLAY

Longing for sexual pleasure is pervasive in society. We live in a very sensual world. As a result, there is a strong pull toward sexual enjoyment and experiences. Furthermore, there seems to be an increased desire to amplify sexual play. Statistics for 2022 indicate that the porn industry is a $100 billion business. It caters to the fantasy life by stimulating sexual play first in the mind and then in a person's life. Furthermore, the porn industry is constructed outside of God's moral constraints. And, thus, it gives the illusion of freedom (you can fantasize in any manner) and pleasure (you can experience visually any type of sexual act). It should not surprise us that pornography destroys relationships and degrades other people and the self. This fixation on sexual play is not relegated to pornography. It is prevalent in movies. The hit movie series Fifty Shades of Grey, based on the popular book trilogy, chronicles sexual play and fantasy. It netted $1.32 billion. One psychologist mused as to why people enjoyed the series: "The book reads like you're being seduced into another world." It caters to fantasy.

This societal predilection shapes individual sexual play. Individuals view sexual play as fulfilling personal enjoyment. It is not viewed as sacred but rather simply a physical act. Furthermore, it is for self rather than the other person. "There is no harm in it," as long as it is consensual. It is simply a night of pleasure. As such, the boundaries of what is acceptable are blurred, if not discarded. This can lead to lifelong consequences, as sexual experiences are compared with previous ones and distortions of beauty and attractiveness become normative. Guilt thus becomes summarily rejected, whereas shame is amplified. It is ironic that the pursuit of sexual freedom ultimately leads to bondage.

In contrast, God encourages sexual play within the confines of marriage. Genesis 2:25 states, "And the man and his wife were both naked and were *not ashamed.*" There was no shame over the naked human body within the marriage covenant. It is God's design for humans. Proverbs 5:18–20 states,

Let your fountain be blessed,
  and rejoice in the wife of your youth,
    a lovely deer, a graceful doe.
Let her breasts fill you at all times with delight;
  be intoxicated always in her love.
Why should you be intoxicated, my son, with a forbidden
woman
  and embrace the bosom of an adulteress?

These verses spotlight a contrast between the worldly notion of sexual play—"embrace the bosom of an adulteress" and godly sexual play—"*rejoice* in the wife of your youth . . . let her breasts *fill you at all times with delight*." The language is not describing sex for means of procreation; it is sexual *pleasure and enjoyment* (delight). It describes sexual play within the marriage covenant. It is freeing. It is fun.

Song of Solomon chronicles sexual play. It is an erotic exchange between two lovers. She delights in his body, "His arms are rods of gold, set with jewels. His body is polished ivory, bedecked with sapphires" (5:14). In response, he longs after her, "Your navel is a rounded bowl that never lacks mixed wine. Your belly is a heap of wheat, encircled with lilies. Your two breasts are like two fawns, twins of a gazelle" (7:2–3). It eventually leads to sexual consummation,

Come, my beloved,
  let us go out into the fields
  and lodge in the villages;
let us go out early to the vineyards
  and see whether the vines have budded,
whether the grape blossoms have opened
  and the pomegranates are in bloom.
There I will give you my love. (7:11–12)

There is no shame or guilt in this exchange. It is portrayed as beautiful. It captures true sexual freedom between a man and a woman within a marriage relationship. There is no guilt in desiring the other person physically.

And there should be no shame in enjoying one's spouse sexually. God grants husbands and wives permission to enjoy sexual play, *with freedom and pleasure*.

As a word of guidance, married couples should communicate honestly and openly about sexual play; otherwise, it can be abused by one individual imposing a preference on another person. When this occurs, guilt and shame can occur even though the sexual play is occurring within the confines of marriage. Both individuals should be free both in the conversation about the sexual play and the sexual play itself.

THE LIFE OF DAVID

David was a man after God's own heart (1 Sam. 13:14). He experienced tremendous highs by slaying Goliath and expanding the nation's borders. He also suffered incredible lows when he had to flee Saul's pursuits and his son Absalom usurped his reign. I enjoy the biblical account of David because it captures the full scope of the human condition.

David experienced both godly play and worldly play, including the devastating effects of the latter. In 2 Samuel 6, we see David enjoying godly play through worship. He was bringing the ark of the covenant into Jerusalem. "And when those who bore the ark of the LORD had gone six steps, he sacrificed an ox and a fattened animal. And David *danced before the* LORD with all his might. And David was wearing a linen ephod. So David and all the house of Israel brought up the ark of the LORD with shouting and with the sound of the horn" (2 Sam. 6:13–15). He was dancing in the presence of God. He was engaging in worshipful play. In this passage, David was playing *within the moral constraints of God's desires*; therefore, he could play with freedom and pleasure.

In this same passage, he was presented with false guilt. His wife, Michal, chastised him for "uncovering himself" and thus dishonoring himself and the kingship (2 Sam. 6:20). She was appealing to *her perceived standards* as to how he should conduct himself. She was wanting him to feel guilty over his actions. Yet, he rebuffs this guilt—"I will celebrate before the LORD. I will make myself yet more contemptible than this, and I will be abased in your eyes" (2 Sam. 6:21–22). He knew his dancing was acceptable in the eyes of the Lord. He knew this form of play was pleasing to God. Therefore, he could fully enjoy it without guilt or shame.

In contrast, and tragically, several years later he succumbed to worldly play by sexually assaulting Bathsheba (2 Sam. 11). She was married to Uriah, one of his mighty men. One night she was bathing on a rooftop. David saw her, summoned her, and then assaulted her. He later had her husband, Uriah, killed to cover up his sexual play. Yet God sent Nathan to rebuke David for his actions. He was overcome with remorse and pleaded for God's mercy.

> Have mercy on me, O God,
>   according to your steadfast love;
> according to your abundant mercy
>   blot out my transgressions.
> Wash me thoroughly from my iniquity,
>   and cleanse me from my sin!
>
> For I know my transgressions,
>   and my sin is ever before me.
> Against you, you only, have I sinned. (Ps. 51:1–4)

He was overcome with guilt because he violated God's moral standard (v. 4). He was also filled with shame over his self-failure (v. 3). In this event, his play, while momentarily seen as freedom and pleasure ("I can do what I want to whom I want for my sexual gratification"), ultimately led to devastation, depression, and personal consequences, including the child dying who was conceived and birthed from this act. Play enjoyed within God's moral standards leads to freedom and pleasure; outside of his standards it leads to guilt and shame, and at times personal, emotional, and physical devastation.

Thankfully, God is a forgiving God. When we respond to guilt by coming to him, he is faithful and just to forgive us (1 John 1:9). Equally, in Christ, we are children of God; therefore, we are rooted in this identity. We might have moments of "self-failure" and thus defeat, but this is not the end of the story. It can lead to hope so that the next time we play, we do so with freedom and pleasure, as God intended.

SUMMARIZING THOUGHTS

God designed play to be beautiful. It should stimulate pleasure and freedom in us. It should be enjoyed with spontaneity and exuberance, and without guilt and shame. To do so requires us to play within the moral guardrails set for us. These guardrails are far apart, leading to an open expanse between them by which to celebrate life. They are not restrictive. On the contrary, they are freeing! The illusion of worldly freedom, however momentarily enticing, appears expansive without borders or edges, but in reality, it is narrow and constricting, resulting in guilt and shame. We should embrace true play as permitted and framed by God, the author and giver of play.

REFLECTION

This chapter requires reflection on our moral compass. It is important to take time and consider what the Bible states in regard to forms of godly play versus worldly play. Furthermore, we must discern and reject the words of well-meaning Christians who attempt to create further hedges around play, leading to false guilt.

1. How does the world esteem play? Why does it esteem play in this manner? What is attractive, even to you, about this form of play?

2. How does God esteem play? Why does he esteem play in this manner? Why is this form of play good for us? What should be attractive to us about this form of play?

3. Think about the tension between worldly play and godly play. How can you take steps toward living within the moral guardrails of godly play?

4. Reflect on a time you experienced false guilt. What was your reaction to it? How can you guard against false guilt that would suffocate liberating play?

5. How are you encouraging godly play in others?

CHAPTER 9

Learning to Lighten Up: Playing at Work

This is the real secret of life—to be completely engaged with what you are doing in the here and now. And instead of calling it work, realize it is play.

—Alan Watts

The current US workplace is experiencing an identity crisis. Gallup conducted a global survey in 2023 and discovered that only 13 percent of workers are engaged in their jobs (Gallup 2023, 30). Engaged is understood as involving fulfillment and enjoyment. This means that roughly 85 percent of workers do not like their jobs. An additional survey in August 2022 revealed that 60 percent are emotionally detached at work, 50 percent feel stressed out, 41 percent are worried, 22 percent are sad, and 18 percent are angry. The reasons for dissatisfaction range from unfair treatment to unreasonable demands.

Companies are demanding more of their workers—longer hours, weekend work, and decreased salaries. Shortly after Elon Musk took over Twitter, he renovated part of the headquarters into hotel rooms. The intent was to allow workers to invest more time at the company. They can work during the day, go get some sleep, then immediately return to work. It is expected that they work 60–80 hours a week. If they resist longer hours, they are asked to leave the company, if not fired. In response to this trend among organizations, individuals are "quietly quitting" their jobs (Gallup 2023, 2). They are choosing to commit to what is stated in their job descriptions, work no more than 40 hours a week, and be free on weekends. Individuals are increasingly becoming fed up with employers demanding more from them.

This contrasts with companies that have incorporated a laxer environment in recent years. Silicon Valley has become known for foosball tables in the hallways, sleeping pods in quiet rooms for employees who need a nap, and flexible work hours, including the ability to work 100 percent remotely. These companies are striving to accommodate the employees, including fostering more work-life balance. In fall 2022, a collection of companies in the United Kingdom experimented with a four-day workweek without any reduction in pay. They discovered there was no decrease in productivity due to this change. Furthermore, employees have been happier and more dedicated to the company. They are considering making this change permanent. The 2022 Gallup survey monetized this tension. Companies with engaged workers experienced 23 percent higher profits than those businesses with low employee morale. Estimates are that employee dissatisfaction costs the world $7.8 trillion in lost productivity per year.

In other words, it pays, financially and emotionally, to foster healthy, enjoyable workplace environments. This chapter is not the solution for every problem within companies. However, it does seek to remedy some of the dissatisfaction. I propose that one solution to employee misery is to allow and incorporate more play into the workplace. Play should not be relegated to nonwork environments and hours. It should be integrated into all of life, including our jobs.

GOD'S ORIGINAL DESIGN FOR WORK

God originally designed work to be pleasurable. At creation, everything was deemed good. This would have included all the activity in the garden of Eden. In Genesis 2:15, it states, "The LORD God took the man and put him in the garden of Eden to work it and keep it." This commission occurs prior to the Fall. Therefore, this task would have been enjoyable to Adam and Eve. It would not have involved the stress and anger reflected in our current jobs. Furthermore, Andrew Spenser argued that "work it and keep it" should be translated "worship and obey," meaning that the primary purpose for work was to honor God (2017, 71). This is linguistically possible in the Hebrew text because the Hebrew word *avodah* in this verse can be translated "work" or "worship." It is used in both capacities in the Old Testament. I believe this word choice is intentional. Even if one maintains the traditional interpretation—that this should be translated "work"—the nuance of the other use, "worship," is present. It is God saying that work should be worshipful. This mindset fosters an integrated life between our relationship with God and our occupations.

Imagine the work environment in the garden. Sin was not present to cause competition between Adam and Eve regarding their work responsibilities. Tending to the land did not lead to depression or burnout. There was no anger over work-life balance. Stress did not occur over a particular quota or specific deadline. Rather, there was perfect enjoyment at doing God's will. Work was deeply satisfying as they tended to the animals and land. It was worshipful. It was meaningful. It was pleasurable. Furthermore, their boss was perfect, literally.

I believe Adam and Eve delighted in caring for God's creation. I also suspect they played. If work was fully enjoyable because sin was absent, is it not reasonable to conclude that they enjoyed moments of pleasure and laughter as they worked in the garden? Is it not possible that they took time to chase each other in the field or toss a vegetable at one another? Can you see Eve hiding from Adam in a spontaneous moment of hide-and-seek? I believe they had permission to fully *enjoy play while working*. I don't believe God administered a nine-to-five schedule. Rather, I suspect he encouraged freedom within their work to worship, reflect, laugh, and play. In my perspective, work prior to the Fall perfectly blended productivity with pleasure and play.

WORK POST-FALL

The reason it is difficult to imagine the above scenario with Adam and Eve is that we have no point of reference. Sin has touched every part of our reality, from personal identity to relationships, including work. Thus, it is impossible to experientially imagine a world where work is fully enjoyable with pleasure and freedom. Sin oppresses our vocations.

In Genesis 3, God stated to Adam,

> Cursed is the ground because of you;
>   in pain you shall eat of it all the days of your life;
> thorns and thistles it shall bring forth for you;
>   and you shall eat the plants of the field.
> By the sweat of your face
>   you shall eat bread,
> till you return to the ground,
>   for out of it you were taken;
> for you are dust,
>   and to dust you shall return." (vv. 17–19)

Because of sin, work is now burdensome. It involves "pain" and "sweat." Joy is elusive at work, a sharp contrast to the state prior to the Fall. The Fall has deeply distorted God's original design for work. Individuals' identities are now rooted in one's vocation rather than one's relationship with God. We are defined by what we do rather than who we are. This has fueled humanistic pursuits, as individuals strive to excel in their workplace, both in terms of position and salary. It is thus becoming increasingly important, if not expected, to climb the corporate ladder. Success in life is defined in terms of one's career.

With the industrial age, work became separated from the home. This is in large part due to the shift from an agrarian society to one of manufacturing. Individuals traveled to their workplaces rather than working on their homestead. This shift resulted in work becoming functional rather than meaningful. Work became a matter of earning a paycheck rather than fulfilling a calling. It was the secularization of vocation. Further, this created a distortion of the employee, as individuals were viewed more as objects than as valued members of the company. This depersonalization amplifies self-centered pursuits, as individuals desire to "take" from their work rather than "give back" to society. It is no wonder that employees experience depression, anger, and sadness at work. When self becomes the focus of one's vocation, it inevitably leads to emptiness and joylessness.

The primary distortion of sin is that the individual becomes the focus rather than God. It makes logical sense then that sin corrupted work by making it about the employee rather than a divine vocational calling, as was the original design by God—"to work it and keep it" or "to worship and obey." Furthermore, the emphasis on productivity drives the employer to pressure the worker to do more, to give more, and to sacrifice more for the company. This mindset does not allow for enjoyment, let alone play. Play would be viewed as superfluous, most certainly not something that contributes to the company but rather costs the organization money. Sin has marred God's original design for work.

GOD DESIRES WORK TO BE MEANINGFUL AND PLEASURABLE

Even though sin has caused upheaval in our approach to work, God still desires that we enjoy it. It is possible to find pleasure in our vocations. The book of Ecclesiastes describes Solomon's pursuit for meaning. He tried to find fulfillment in wisdom, wealth, and every form of indulgence. Within this book, the author faced this tension between work as meaningless and work as pleasurable.

He stated in Ecclesiastes 2:18–23,

> I *hated* all my toil in which I toil under the sun, seeing that I must *leave it to the man who will come after me*, and who knows whether he will be wise or a fool? Yet he will be *master of all for which I toiled* and used my wisdom under the sun. This also is vanity. So I turned about and gave my heart up to *despair* over all the toil of my labors under the sun, because sometimes a person who has toiled with wisdom and knowledge and skill must *leave everything to be enjoyed by someone who did not toil for it*. This also is vanity and a great evil. What has a man from all the toil and striving of heart with which he

toils beneath the sun? For *all his days are full of sorrow*, and *his work is a vexation*. Even in the night *his heart does not rest*. This also is vanity. (emphasis mine)

The italicized words vividly describe the impact of the Fall on work. The author "hated" his work. It produced "despair." It was "full of sorrow" and "vexation." His heart was restless. This passage describes work under the curse of sin. For many, this is your work experience. The italicized phrases describe reasons for this frustration—the author was working for the benefit of someone else. In this case, it was his successor. He was a tool for another person's enjoyment. In many respects, this captures the essence of the modern work environment—work is for the benefit of the company, not the individual. There is often no personal meaning in our work. It leads to emptiness—meaninglessness.

There is a sharp contrast in the next verse. The author continued, "There is nothing better for a person than that he should eat and drink and find enjoyment in his toil. This also, I saw, is from the hand of God" (2:24). Rather than the enjoyment going to someone else, the worker should personally find enjoyment. It can be meaningful to the individual. This is reiterated in Ecclesiastes 3:13, "… everyone should eat and drink and take pleasure in all his toil—this is God's gift to man." God desires for individuals to enjoy work—to find pleasure. When an individual finds meaning and purpose at work, not for someone else, but as an expression of their calling, it produces pleasure. It is possible even under the effects of the Fall.

This perspective enables a person to play. When work is unbundled from ambition, productivity, monetary gain, and career advancement, a person can discover pleasure through work, nurture meaningful relationships, and find true satisfaction in their toil. This creates the conditions to play at work—to enjoy banter with colleagues, interdepartmental games or friendly competitions, and retreats where play is the mechanism for community building. It is possible if we choose to embrace a different perspective. It is possible if employers create space and permission for play. Furthermore, it is good for the company and can potentially produce higher profits.

BENEFITS OF PLAY AT WORK

This section explores the various benefits of play at work. My hope is that you will imagine a different reality at your job—that it is possible to work hard while also incorporating play. I encourage you to not simply read these pages as "that would be nice to see work in that way" but rather "I am going to take small steps toward incorporating play at work."

Play Enhances Productivity

I commented earlier that engagement at work leads to increased productivity. Play also increases productivity. A 2018 study by Brigham Young University researchers revealed that workers who played a collaborative video game together experienced a 20 percent increase in productivity when compared to individuals who participated in a traditional team-building activity (Keith et al. 2018). It led to a great sense of cohesion and community. Play also increases innovation at one's work (Brower 2019). It fosters curiosity, creativity, and problem-solving capabilities—essential components of work productivity. As Tracey Brower stated, "Playfulness is linked to humor and the distance from 'Ha Ha' and 'Ah Ha' is short" (Brower 2019).

The intangible but essential skills of critical thinking and exploration are innately connected to our being made in the image of God. God uniquely designed us to be curious and creative. He desires that these qualities be exercised in our work. Exodus 31:1–5 states,

> The LORD said to Moses, "See, I have called by name Bezalel the son of Uri, son of Hur, of the tribe of Judah, and I have filled him with the Spirit of God, with ability and intelligence, with knowledge and all craftsmanship, to devise artistic designs, to work in gold, silver, and bronze, in cutting stones for setting, and in carving wood, to work in every craft."

Bezalel's skills were an expression of God's Spirit in him (v. 3). Being "filled" by God's Spirit resulted in his "ability and intelligence" (v. 3). Walter Kaiser Jr. described these skills as "gifts of the Holy Spirit" (1990,

475).There is a relationship between our being made in the image of God and our problem-solving capabilities. Being made in the image of God and infused with God's Spirit uniquely allowed Bezalel to create or "devise artistic designs" (v. 4). Furthermore, his work as a craftsman is a calling (vv. 2–3). It is not for functional purposes—to make a living—but as an embodiment of God's purposes in his life. He was not called to be a priest, but he was called to be an artist.

If our intelligence, knowledge, and creativity are embodiments and expressions of being made in the image of God, and for Christians an expression of God's Spirit in us, should we not find ways to enhance these qualities at work? Why should these divinely embedded qualities be relegated to hobbies or inventive roles? They should be unleashed in the workplace. Research affirms that play enhances these qualities. As such, it would be beneficial for companies to permit play and workers to engage in play as a means toward greater work productivity. For the Christian, this approach to work also equips one's calling and flourishes it. In essence, we should embrace the connection between God's desire for meaning at work and its enhancement through play.

Play Encourages Workplace Trust

It is not uncommon for fellow workers to be viewed as colleagues and nothing more. The transient nature of work further suppresses one's desire to cultivate deep friendships at one's workplace; no one knows how long another person will be there. Play counteracts this disconnect and fosters trust between individuals, even if trust was not the intentional aim. "Sharing laughter and fun can foster empathy, compassion, trust, and intimacy with others" (Robinson et al. 2023). When you laugh and joke with another person, you feel a relational connection. You share an experience that becomes stored as a positive memory in your mind. It leads to a greater propensity to share more openly with that person. In many respects, play demonstrates vulnerability. It is a form of safe risk.

The Fall stirs feelings of competition and comparison (Gal. 5:19–21), particularly at work. It leads to unhealthy relationships, even volatility, as we strive to outdo and outmaneuver one another for personal gain and promotion. The relationship between Saul and David embodies these sinful expressions. Saul was David's boss. Yet he became jealous of David over his successes, particularly when the people esteemed him more, as expressed in their song "Saul has struck down his thousands, and David his ten thousands" (1 Sam. 18:7; see 18:6–11). It permanently dissolved the relationship, leading to Saul attempting to kill David on numerous occasions. This relationship contrasts with David and Jonathan, Saul's eldest son, seen in the same chapter. If Saul was David's boss, Jonathan was his coworker (both served in the military). Despite David's successes, Jonathan, who rightfully could have been jealous since he was heir to the throne, bonded with him—"the soul of Jonathan was knit to the soul of David, and Jonathan loved him as his own soul" (1 Sam. 18:1). Trust and intimacy were forged between them. There are no biblical references to David and Jonathan playing. However, I suspect they shared moments of laughter and enjoyment as they served the nation.

When I served as a pastor, I often utilized short games as part of leadership meetings. They were usually connected to some decision—a way to think about a problem. They were moments of levity while we made decisions about church strategy and congregational needs. Yet the unintended result of playing games together was camaraderie. Even if that game was competitive, it led to a naturalness, an openness, that then translated over to the formal agenda items. The moment of play had the larger benefit of making the entire meeting more enjoyable. I could have viewed games as optional—"if we have time in the meeting," but I believed laughter and enjoyment would have greater dividends than accomplishing the agenda items in the quickest and most efficient way possible. Trust is an intangible quality in the workplace, yet it is critically necessary for employee happiness and satisfaction. Play enhances this happiness and satisfaction by cultivating trust rather than envy among those around us.

Play Increases Worker Longevity

God desires that we commit wholeheartedly to whatever we do. "Whatever you do, work heartily, as for the Lord and not for men, knowing that from the Lord you will receive the inheritance as your reward. You are serving the Lord Christ" (Col. 3:23–24). This verse affirms that work should be an act of worship ("whatever we do"). Ultimately, our focus should be on God rather than the company. It can be challenging to maintain this perspective in a humanistic world, where employees are oftentimes viewed in terms of how much money they bring to the company. As a result, our worshipful perspectives can erode in cutthroat environments. I believe that a perspective realignment toward work as worship would enhance longevity. We would see our vocations as places of mission and meaning rather than sources of a paycheck.

It is unreasonable to expect non-Christian companies to embrace a Christian worldview. But for Christian companies, particularly owners and managers in those organizations, it is necessary, as a spiritual act, to think through how one can foster conditions to allow individuals "to commit wholeheartedly." Obviously, there are numerous ways to accomplish this—fair treatment, work-home balance, and equitable compensation. Germane to this book is the topic of play. Creating conditions of play within one's organizations can help the overall workplace environment and enhance spiritual vibrancy. It can create pleasurable work atmospheres that are more easily conducive to worker commitment.

In the secular space, Silicon Valley has created fun workspaces to increase worker longevity and reduce turnover. Turnover is costly to the organization by increasing transition and training costs. Research indicates that employee turnover cost companies $2.4 trillion in 2021 (Worqdrive 2022). In addition to reducing turnover, play reduces employee dissatisfaction. Most individuals are change averse. The prospect of changing jobs every few years is not attractive. For these reasons, companies are increasingly adding arcade games, pool tables, and relaxation spaces to keep workers engaged and committed. In other words, they are intentionally incorporating environments for play into their spaces to increase employee enjoyment. They rightfully understand that a playful work environment not only improves employee satisfaction and engagement but also promotes worker longevity.

I believe secular companies should not lead the way in terms of workplace enjoyment and stability. Rather, Christian organizations should be the pioneers by fostering vibrant, flourishing places where workers can work hard and play hard. I have a Christian friend who started a financial investment firm. He built it from the ground up, beginning in his garage. When the firm grew, he rented space in a business complex. As part of the workspace design, he incorporated an open floor plan with a coffee bar, casual chairs, and an area for table tennis. Initially I was surprised. I questioned whether clients would enjoy investing their money in a place that encouraged casualness and play. Would they think that the consultants were not taking their jobs seriously and thus the investments? The opposite occurred. The overall returns in the firm increased. The clients were happy, but more importantly, the workers were happy. They had an environment that fostered playful interactions and enjoyment. They had freedom to play at their jobs. The result was a greater commitment to the company and the work.

Play Improves Homelife (and Transitions to Homelife)

In our digital world, work is always accessible and always present. This is the new reality. It is not likely to change. For remote workers, it is easy to feel that your home is synonymous with work. Therefore, it can negatively impact your ability to enjoy nonworking hours. For others, you are never fully off from work in that your job requires you to check emails in the evening or attend to projects. Others find that work is incredibly stressful. As a result, it spills over to homelife in that you need to process the frustrations of the day before you can begin to rest. These realities can easily lead to burnout because individuals feel work dominates their lives. They live to work rather than work to live.

Play at work can improve each of these scenarios. It fosters enjoyment that then reduces the sense that work consumes our lives. Rather than begrudging work, work becomes part of your life rhythm rather than strictly compartmentalized. It makes logical sense. If you enjoyed work, it would not be difficult to engage in it. Even more so, if work also consisted of play, it would be life-giving at times. It would be pleasurable rather than simply functional.

Furthermore, being able to play allows us to transition better to homelife because there is less of a need to demarcate the two. Stress would be reduced, resulting in less need for decompression at home. A person can more easily transition to homelife, naturally and freely, because the built-up frustrations of the workday no longer need release. This is the benefit of play. The playful pockets throughout one's day serve as a pressure relief valve. They allow you to breathe, laugh, and smile.

Work can be challenging and frustrating. The curse on humanity's toil described in Genesis 3 is a reality for all of us. We experience difficulties, workplace gossip, employer abuse, and coworker manipulation. The impact of mental health issues, emptiness, and stress further points to the plague on humankind. Yet, there is hope. Proverbs 17:22 states, "A cheerful heart is good medicine" (NIV). Play can buoy the soul during difficulties. The psalmist states, "You have turned for me my mourning into dancing; you have loosed my sackcloth and clothed me with gladness" (Ps. 30:11). God can infuse our hearts with pleasure and enjoyment, even in stressful moments. This is equally true in our workplaces. By incorporating more playful moments at work, we might just find our workplaces more enjoyable, which can then result in healthier, more vibrant homes.

Play Increases Our Enjoyment of Work

We would look forward to work if it involved regular moments of play. There are numerous times throughout the year when my team ventures outside the office and plays. I remember one outing when we went to Mr. Stumpy's. It is a venue where groups can reserve a time to throw axes. There are various pits set up around the room. Someone trains the groups on proper throwing form. You then can divide up into groups or pairs and throw axes against one another (not at one another). It was an incredible experience for our team. No one was particularly good at throwing axes. Therefore, we made fun of each another. When we were fortunate enough to hit the target, we hollered and screamed. There were also several close calls where the axe came flying back at someone. The entire afternoon was filled with enjoyment because we played. This experience bonded us together as a team. It fostered trust and intimacy that carried over for weeks. We were more natural with one another in the hallways. We stopped to chat in the kitchen rather than immediately grabbing a cup of coffee and rushing back to our computer.

When the event was originally announced, I immediately shared it with my family. "You are not going to believe what we are doing as a team. Axe throwing!" My family was immediately jealous of my work, "I would love to be part of that team." I looked forward to that event. I was excited to go to work on the day of the outing *because we were going to go play*. Yet, the interesting part of this experience is that I enjoyed not only the actual day of the event but the following days and weeks. Even though subsequent days consisted of seemingly mundane work, I was looking forward to it because of the shared experience of play. The mundane was interrupted with moments of laughter and someone saying, "Axes would be a good way to deal with this situation." We joked about the event, but we also chuckled at other circumstances. This event opened up communication and banter. We relaxed more. We enjoyed work more. And we began to play more, naturally and more frequently, in the normal rhythms of the day, because we were given permission to play.

God instructs us to "Go, eat your bread with joy, and drink your wine with a merry heart, for God has already approved what you do" (Eccl. 9:7) and further says:

> Behold, what I have seen to be good and fitting is to eat and drink and find enjoyment in all the toil with which one toils under the sun the few days of his life that God has given him, for this is his lot. Everyone also to whom God has given wealth and possessions and power to enjoy them, and to accept his lot and rejoice in his toil—this is the gift of God. (Eccl. 5:18–19)

We are called to enjoy life. These words are not reserved for only leisure moments but all moments, including our work ("toil"). In fact, the author motivates us to play by reminding us that our days are "few" in this life—this is our "lot." Yet we should not begrudge it but rather accept it. In doing so, we can rejoice. The ability to enjoy work is a gift from God. Even as we experience the consequences of sin at work, God provides us with the ability to enjoy it. This is God's grace.

A Reminder

It is possible to read this section on the benefits of play and presume it is up to you to remedy work woes. This is not the case. We have a comforter, the Holy Spirit, promised to us (John 14:16–17). We can call on him for help. When we do, God promises to be with us. Perhaps you find your work environment so oppressive and unhealthy that you cannot even imagine the possibility of enjoyment, let alone play. In such situations, ask God to give you eyes to see a fellow coworker with whom you can enjoy some play, or eyes to see the humor in a situation, even if you must laugh only to yourself. Or ask God to show you ways in which you can peel away physically and emotionally, even for a moment, to enjoy life, perhaps during lunch or a break. It is important to remember that ultimately play is a gift from God, not something we do in our human effort. God wants us to play, even if our work situation is challenging. It is possible in his strength (Phil. 4:13).

A NOVEL CONCEPT: CHRISTIAN WORK

Since sin impacted the world, including work, through the Fall, and Christ redeemed the world through the cross, it makes logical sense that it is possible to redeem work. Christ came to redeem all things. This includes work. Therefore, it is possible and necessary to imagine a different workplace reality. I imagine a place where everyone is treated with dignity and respect as image bearers of God rather than as mere tools. I imagine a place where humans are allowed to flourish rather than wither. I imagine work communities where genuine human interaction occurs and deep friendships are not only formed but are the norm. I imagine places where work is meaningful and satisfying rather than monetized. I imagine organizations where trust is abundant between bosses and workers, and among coworkers. I imagine companies where productivity involves curiosity and creativity that produces self-worth and organizational worth. And I imagine institutions that promote play, intentionally and generously, for the pleasure and enjoyment of their workers. This environment would be restorative. It would lead to human flourishing. It would allow workers to "worship and obey" with enthusiasm and freedom. Rather than wait for these environments to be fostered, perhaps we should take the first step toward making them a reality by proactively redeeming our little corners of our workplaces.

SUMMARIZING THOUGHTS

Play is the God-given ability and permission to fully enjoy moments in life as God intended, with freedom and pleasure. This is often easier to do in nonwork settings, where we enjoy more control over our lives. We can choose when to play and how to play. At work, we are constrained by our occupational demands and organizational expectations. As a result, we typically feel restricted and thus unable to play. I would argue that play is possible even at work if we allow ourselves to imagine the playful possibilities. It might look different for each person depending on your work situation, yet it can become a reality. This God-given ability is not dependent on employer approval. It is a gift from God. Therefore, it is not only possible, it is achievable if you dare to imagine it and seize it.

REFLECTION

Life is too short. We spend at minimum one-third of our lives at work. We sometimes see our coworkers more than our families. Considering this reality, should we not begin to enjoy work more fully and more richly? Take some time to reflect on how you can incorporate play into your work.

1. Describe your work environment in five words. What qualities characterize your job situation?

2. Imagine your ideal work setting. What would this look like in terms of relationships, meaning, and enjoyment?

3. Create a list of possible ways you can infuse play into your everyday work situation. This might involve something small (laughing with a coworker during a break) or something large (planning a post-work dinner or work outing).

4. If you are an owner or manager, how can you intentionally and generously create conditions for play and give permission to play, in your company or to those you oversee?

5. Ask God for perspective, a willingness to play, and the grace to enjoy play at work, especially if you are in a difficult work setting.

CHAPTER 10

Learning to Embrace Discomfort: Playing in the Pain of Life

Oh, taste and see that the LORD is good!
Blessed is the man who takes refuge in him!
                                        —Psalm 34:8

The scariest moment of my life occurred on December 6, 2013. My wife and I were shopping at Yorktown Center in Lombard, Illinois. Our daughter was browsing the stores with a friend, while our son tagged along by our sides. We were in the Marshalls department store. My phone rang in my pocket. The caller ID indicated it was Elmhurst Memorial Hospital. It was my family doctor. He immediately started asking if I felt tired. He wanted to know about my appetite. I responded, "I feel great." At this point, I began to grow concerned. He proceeded to tell me that my blood work came back as part of a routine physical. It indicated a significantly elevated white blood cell count. Based on the pathology report, they suspected I had leukemia.

My wife was looking at me, wondering who was on the phone. I mouthed that it was the doctor and he believed I had cancer. Her face went pale. We were not sure how to respond to this news. It was shocking. It was surreal. It was like someone punched us in the gut. I grew quiet. The ride home was painfully slow, as if time stood still. Our daughter was laughing with her friend in the backseat, unaware of the news. When we returned home after dropping her friend off, we shared what the doctor suspected. As a family, we were devastated. There were long hugs and many tears. We did not know what the future held. At that point, we were not certain as to the severity of the cancer. We did not know what the next steps would be in terms of treatment. That night was the longest I could remember. I barely slept, tossing and turning the entire night. My wife didn't sleep at all. I vividly remember the myriad thoughts racing through my mind. They were the same ones many people have in this same situation. Will I be able to walk my daughter down the aisle? Will I see my son graduate? Is my wife going to be OK financially? How long do I have left?

The next morning was a Saturday. We didn't know when we would be able to see a specialist. It ended up being several days. The waiting game is always the hardest. You have no information, and your mind drifts toward the worst-case scenario. It is like time stopped, but your mind is going two hundred miles per hour. We did not know how to even begin processing this news.

It snowed overnight. It was the first snowfall of the year. The yard was covered in a beautiful white blanket. The kids wanted to go play in the snow. We thought it would be a good distraction for them. My wife bundled herself and the kids up and went out on the back porch. Since I was not certain as to the severity of the diagnosis, we thought it best for me to stay inside. I watched through the back door for quite a while as they threw snowballs at one another.

As numerous thoughts swirled around my head, I remember clearly thinking in that moment, "I might have cancer, but I am going to live, no matter how long I have left." I quickly threw on my winter gear, opened the door, made a snowball, and threw it at the one of the kids. My wife asked if I thought that was wise. I shared with her that I did not want the cancer to define me. And so I played! I am deeply thankful I did. It showed me that it was possible to still live, and even play, after receiving horrific news.

Thankfully, I was informed several days later that I have CLL, the milder version of leukemia. I undergo frequent checkups, but to this day I have not needed treatment. I know that others have not been as fortunate. I do not wish to minimize your pain if you have been diagnosed with or have lost a loved one to cancer or some other tragedy. Three years later, I would receive another diagnosis, that of bladder cancer. The tumor was removed, but I still receive checkups for that one as well. I joke that I am an overachiever and I guess that includes all areas, including cancer. The reason for this personal story is to share that it is possible to play in the pain of life, and to affirm that I understand a bit of what you might be going through as you wrestle with playing in the pain of life.

HOW AM I ABLE TO PLAY IN THE PAIN OF LIFE?

This is a question that I have thought about over the past ten years. As I reflect upon this season in my life, I believe I have played more since my diagnosis than I did in the twenty years before it. Yes, I had moments of laughter and happiness. But something happened in me that evening that compelled me to squeeze every ounce out of life. I believe the answer lies in the following paragraphs. It is the reason I can play with true freedom and pleasure.

Priorities

When I got the diagnosis of cancer, I immediately prioritized what was important in my life. There was some stripping of trivial pursuits. I say "some" because I am still human. I am still ambitious. I still have moments of frustration and anger. I still strive to excel in everything I do. But in that moment, there was a shedding of some wasted pursuits—the desire to pour myself into work for accolades, the goal to become wealthy, and the choosing of ministry needs over my family. I believe many people come to this aha moment when they retire. It is the realization that work is never going to be as loyal to you as you were to it. In some respects, it is then too late. They would have missed out on so many opportunities. Thus, for me, cancer crystallized at age forty-two what was critical in my life—faith, family, and investing in things of consequence. In this sense, cancer has been a gift. It has enabled me to enjoy freedom and pleasure while living with cancer.

Amos 6:13 addresses "you who rejoice in Lo-debar, who say, 'Have we not by our own strength captured Karnaim for ourselves?'" The word *Lo-debar* means "nothing." This passage is challenging those who put their joy in trivial, unimportant matters to see their futility. The author of Psalm 90:12 implores God to "teach us to number our days that we may get a heart of wisdom." This is what cancer forced me to do—to peer into the future and remember that this life is fleeting, and thus, to appreciate every day. No one knows how many days we have in this life; therefore, why not enjoy it? Ecclesiastes 8:14–17 in the New Living Translation states,

> And this is not all that is meaningless in our world. In this life, good people are often treated as though they were wicked, and wicked people are often treated as though they were good. This is so meaningless!

> So I recommend having fun, because there is nothing better for people in this world than to eat, drink, and enjoy life. That way they will experience some happiness along with all the hard work God gives them under the sun.

> In my search for wisdom and in my observation of people's burdens here on earth, I discovered that there is ceaseless activity, day and night. I realized that no one can discover everything God is doing under the sun. Not even the wisest people discover everything, no matter what they claim.

Verse 15 encourages the reader to have "fun . . . enjoy life . . . and experience some happiness." This passage refers to the "meaninglessness in our world" and "the burdens here on earth." (vv. 14, 16). From a human perspective, I can think of nothing seemingly more "meaningless" than cancer. And any ongoing pain that is experienced is truly a "burden." Verse 17 states that "no one can discover everything God is doing under the sun." I don't fully know what God is doing with leukemia. I can't even pretend to imagine what God might be doing in your pain. Like you, I have had deep moments of anguish, anxiety, and frustration. Many times, I wake up thinking about it. There is an emotional toll to pain. Yet, I also know God is doing something in me, because he is neither passive nor cruel. He is active and good. This is one reason I believe Solomon encourages the reader to play. If much of life is meaningless and it is ultimately futile to understand all of God's plans, then why not enjoy life? Rely on his grace by trusting him for the future, but also play! The alternative is to fret and search for something that might never be fully known. I choose play!

For me, cancer has been a mechanism to great joy. It is not because I have learned some great mystery of God's purposes, or that I like having cancer. I don't and I wish I didn't have it. However, cancer has been useful to remind me of the richness and necessity of play, as a means to affirm that there is always more to life than the pain. I have learned to choose to play with my family over other trivial and inferior pursuits. I have learned that life it too short not to play. And I have learned that cancer does not define my identity, thus allowing me to play.

Goodness

I had to reaffirm and redefine goodness.

Goodness is typically understood in terms of comfort; thus we feel we cannot play when life is hard. Life is not good (comfortable); therefore I cannot enjoy it. In other words, we attach play to our mood—if it is up, we can play; if it is down, we cannot play. The above poem contrasts with a journalist I read, who commented, "Why me? Why did I have to get cancer and not the abuser down the street?" This is a statement about goodness. It is not good to experience pain. It seems unfair. Pain questions God's goodness. Honestly, I had some similar thoughts, thinking, "I committed myself to ministry. Why would God allow me to get cancer?"

Psalm 27:13–14 states, "I believe that I shall look upon the goodness of the LORD in the land of the living! Wait for the LORD; be strong, and let your heart take courage; wait for the LORD!" These verses highlight the tension between pain and faith in God's goodness. While there is belief, the psalmist needs courage. It is the quintessential, "I believe; help my unbelief!" (Mark 9:24). Psalm 34:8 declares, "Oh, taste and see that the LORD is good! Blessed is the man who takes refuge in him!" Goodness is not always connected to peace and comfort; in these verses it is during pain—"take refuge."

It is not easy having cancer. There are times I feel fatigued, and I worry if the cancer has turned for the worse. The days leading up to my appointments are restless ones. Waiting for the blood results to come in makes my palms sweat. These moments do not seem "good." However, they do drive me to God's strength and peace. They force me to affirm God's goodness beyond comfort, even if I don't see that goodness. Goodness in God's economy lies deeper than the external. It is found in richer, more secure qualities—God's security, salvation, grace, strength, and peace. These are the immutable qualities of the Christian life. This is refreshing. If goodness were defined by the externals, God in essence would become a benefactor. And if God became a benefactor, he would cease to be God. We would become the focus rather than the Almighty One.

Goodness is rooted in God's character, not our comfort. Romans 8:28 states, "We know that for those who love God all things work together for *good*, for those who are called according to his purpose." Goodness in this passage is directly connected to God's attributes and ultimate purposes. In these verses, Paul is referring to our new position in Christ as the "firstborn" and our future hope in "glory" (vv. 29–30). Because of this hope, we can affirm confidently that nothing "will be able to separate us from the love of God in Christ Jesus our Lord" (v. 39). Yet, in the midst of these verses, we find pain. In verse 26, there is an affirmation of "our weakness", and later in verse 35, our suffering from "tribulation, or distress, or persecution, or famine, or nakedness, or danger, or sword" (v. 35). This passage affirms that God's goodness coexists in and with pain.

We can play in our present moments, even during pain, because we know that God will work everything out for his good purposes. For me, I believe the good purposes include my formation into more of Christ's image because the pain drives me to him. For me, I believe the good purposes are the deepening of my relationship with Christ, knowing that my identity in him will transcend the pain and even death. For me, I believe the good purposes are a further tasting of his love and mercy that would not be possible if I were comfortable all the time. If goodness is defined in terms of something deeper than external matters and physical comforts, then I can truly play, because my core identity (being in relationship with Christ) is immovable, even if my physical body is experiencing a hurricane.

My father passed away unexpectedly, shortly after turning sixty-five. He was undergoing a routine hernia operation. During the procedure, he suffered a massive stroke. He never woke up. Within a few days, we disconnected life support, and he passed away peacefully into the arms of Jesus. The next few weeks produced numerous feelings—shock, anger, grief, and sadness. The emotions would come in waves without any warning. My daughter was four years old at the time. Therefore, she did not fully understand the significance or ramifications of death. Yet on numerous occasions over those few weeks, she wanted to play. Since she was young, she needed playmates, which was typically me and my wife. Therefore, we found ourselves playing—in the back yard running around, playing a game, or laughing at a joke. We would not have chosen to play given the circumstances. But her innocence and spontaneity pulled us into it. Playing during this time was very helpful to us. It lifted us out of our grief for a moment. It reminded us that there was so much to live for—that even though my father had passed away, we were still rich as a family. Play provided hope for us.

Future Hope

God is outside of time; therefore, he can see everything. Isaiah 46:9–10 declares, "I am God, and there is no other; I am God, and there is none like me, declaring the end from the beginning and from ancient times things not yet done, saying, 'My counsel shall stand, and I will accomplish all my purpose.'" God is not surprised by future events. He is fully aware of the future pain that we will experience. As a result, he can be fully present in our current suffering. His sovereignty over time enables him to provide sufficient grace and strength in the moment. In reference to the defiance of nations, Psalm 2:4 states, "He who sits in the heavens laughs; the Lord holds them in derision." He laughs because the nations do not affirm his authority over life. This same posture can be applied to pain. He laughs at any sentiment that doubts his control. Is God sovereign if he allowed this pain to occur? Why did he allow this to happen? If he is sovereign, can he be good, since I am suffering? These are valid questions if we define goodness in an earthly manner—God is to make us happy. God's laughter should not be viewed as unsympathetic. He weeps with us (John 11:35). His laughter is instead a response to the questioning of his authority. To fully play as Christians, therefore, it is essential to see other possibilities for our suffering than God's capriciousness or impotence.

Suffering Can Lead to Something Greater in This World

Sarah was barren for most of her life. Yet God granted her a child when she was ninety. In response to Isaac's birth, Sarah said, "God has made laughter for me; everyone who hears will laugh over me" (Gen. 21:6). Identity for women in this ancient culture was tied to motherhood. For a woman not to have a child was tantamount to being cursed. It was interpreted as God withholding his blessing from that person. Sarah would have experienced tremendous shame and embarrassment because of her barrenness.

This suffering produced something more meaningful for her in the future. In the moment, she did not see it, but in time, she saw God's provision for her. This caused her to laugh. I imagine this laughter was not the type expressed when hearing a joke. Rather, it was a laughter that communicated, "Wow. I did not see that coming. Oh, how wrong I was to doubt God's plans. He certainly surprised me." It was a laugh of joy. It captured a playful heart in realizing God's disclosed plan that had been hidden for years.

This can be deeply meaningful for us. During pain, it is challenging to see any hope. We only see the discomfort, disruption, and despair. Imagining any good coming from the pain seems ridiculous. Yet, if we truly affirm God's sovereignty and goodness, we ground our perspective and emotions in hope that he will bring something greater from it, even if the pain is not removed. It might be character development. It might compel us to be a witness of grace lived through pain. It might be a ministry opportunity that was opened because of this crucible moment. This hope, even if it seems impossible, permits us to enjoy this present moment. It frees us to play by allowing God to control and determine the future. The alternative is bathing ourselves in the misery of the pain, which only paralyzes us from any enjoyment. It is a fist wrapped around our pain, in frustration and anger, shaking at God. Trusting God for the possibility of good coming from current suffering can allow us to "laugh" today rather than wait till the time that we see the good realized.

In the series *The Lord of the Rings: The Rings of Power*, the elven king Gil-galad, when facing possible extinction of the elves, says to Elrond,

"Hope is never mere . . . even when it is meager. When all other senses sleep, the eye of hope is first to waken, last to shut" (Doble 2022). This should be true of our faith in God's purposes when experiencing pain. It is this hope that allows us to rest in the moment, smile in the moment, and even play in the moment. It affirms that this pain is not the last chapter.

Suffering Will Cease in This World for Something Greater in the Next World

The belief for many in this world is that this world is it. There is nothing beyond this life. Sometimes I believe Christians embrace this worldview even though we affirm the afterlife. We respond to our suffering in such a way that seems to place our hope only in this world, not recognizing our eventual eternal home.

In reference to our future hope, Jeremiah prophesied, "Then shall the young women rejoice in the dance, and the young men and the old shall be merry. I will turn their mourning into joy; I will comfort them, and give them gladness for sorrow" (Jer. 31:13). Our mourning is temporary. It will one day cease. It is not permanent. A future day of dancing, celebration, and rejoicing awaits. If this is our future hope, is it not possible that we can dance and rejoice today *in light of this certainty*? It is like learning a cancer treatment has been discovered that is 100 percent effective even though you have not yet been cured. You would dance at the knowledge of future healing, and thus could dance today.

I believe God knows the human tendency to get dragged into a black hole during pain. As a result, he has provided ample passages that declare our eventual hope. "He will yet fill your mouth with *laughter*, and your lips with shouting" (Job 8:21). "Blessed are you who are hungry now, for you shall be satisfied. Blessed are you who weep now, for you shall *laugh*" (Luke 6:21). I love the emphasis on laughter in these verses. It is a vivid description of delight and play. I imagine that God intentionally utilized this word in these passages that describe present suffering to remind us that this suffering will one day give way to play. We will laugh and not weep. We will play and not suffer. It is the quintessential happy ending. These verses cause me to believe that there will be play in heaven. These passages seem to indicate such—there will be "laughing." If true, play should embody our lives today. It is a form of practice for our eventual interactions in glory.

We can play because we have knowledge that the future will be quite different, even if that future is beyond this world. One of the challenging realities of living in a humanistic world is that our worldview is influenced by it. Rather than sojourners (1 Peter 2:11) in this world, we begin to settle as permanent residents. We are like the Israelites who grew accustomed to Egypt (and longed to return to Egypt) when the promised land awaited them. C. S. Lewis stated in *The Weight of Glory*,

> We are half-hearted creatures, fooling about with drink and sex and ambition when infinite joy is offered us, like an ignorant child who wants to go on making mud pies in a slum because he cannot imagine what is meant by the offer of a holiday at the sea. We are far too easily pleased. (2001, 26)

Our eyes should be fixed on our future hope even though we live in this present reality with all its pain and suffering. Peter, who suffered for his faith, stated, "Instead, be very glad—for these trials make you partners with Christ in his suffering, so that you will have the wonderful joy of seeing his glory when it is revealed to all the world" (1 Peter 4:13 NLT). There can be joy in the present moment in light of the promise of future glory. Proverbs 31:25 salutes the godly woman: "She is clothed with strength and dignity, and she laughs without fear of the future" (NLT). This ability to laugh in the present arises out of a deep faith that trusts God for the future. It recognizes that ultimately all of life will be declared good, including our pain, not because the pain itself is good but because what is produced in us is good.

My wife has a dear friend whose father-in-law passed away. He was a strong Christian. It was during Christmastime. Following the passing of their loved one, my wife's friend and her family chose to go out and look at Christmas lights. This was an activity that he enjoyed doing each year. To honor his memory, they chose to play. It reminded them of previous memories while also aiding in their grief. Play provided comfort. Yet this play was preeminently possible because they knew that he was no longer in pain but rather experiencing the hope of glory in Christ.

A Radical Perspective: Playing in the Midst of Pain

Some might ask how one can play during pain. It seems detached from reality. This would be true without the hope that God is working out something greater in us and for us. To play in the moment requires faith and trust. It is focused on the future while remaining fully present in the moment. It is grabbing hold of our future hope while living in our present reality, even if that reality involves pain.

The challenge is that we live in a world that cherishes control and predictability. In the West, we dislike ambiguity, confusion, and mystery. In fact, it makes us highly uncomfortable. This influences how we approach Scripture and life. We read the Bible with the aim of mastering it through Bible studies, exegetical guides, and theological works. Similarly, we desire to *know* what God is doing in life. The unknown agitates us. Eastern culture tends to embrace mystery. For example, in the rabbinic tradition, they have the posture of enthusiasm when they come across a section of Scripture they do not understand. "They dance because they are so excited that there is something God is going to use in their life later on. And they don't understand it now, but they are excited for the day that God reveals it to them" (Solomon and Billings 2016). The unknown frustrates many of us because we want to know and determine the future. It would benefit us greatly if we embraced this rabbinic perspective that says we can celebrate in the midst of the unknown. It is a radical perspective to enjoy, to celebrate, to play through pain because God will one day reveal the ultimate purpose for it. This is not the most comfortable posture. However, it is one of freedom that can lead to play and pleasure by releasing the incessant desire to know and control. It is a mindset of discovery in what God is doing in life, even in the hardest moments.

What I am proposing here is not a dismissive mindset that ignores or downplays the pain. Rather, it is one that sits deeply in it—acknowledging it and lamenting it. Yet it also sees that this pain is not purposeless. In God's economy, pain has purpose to it, even if it is unknown. For many, freedom would be found in the unknown becoming known. Yet that places confidence in the knowledge (and thus one's control) rather than in the one who truly knows and can control. True freedom is found by resting in the one who can not only determine the outcome of the pain but reveal the purpose for it. Such a mindset creates the conditions for true, liberating play.

While I was talking on the phone with my doctor on that frightening night, a couple walked past me. It was at the exact moment my doctor was giving me the name of an oncologist in downtown Chicago. To write it down, I repeated it back once to confirm, "Dr. Rodriguez." This couple was probably ten feet away and immediately looked back at me with puzzled expressions. I was in a busy store, so I had retreated to a more isolated section. I was also talking quietly, as I am not one to broadcast my news. Roughly five minutes later, they came up to my wife and me. They asked me, "Did you say Dr. Rodriguez?" We confirmed the name and said nothing more. They then proceeded to explain to us that their twenty-five-year-old son had been diagnosed with leukemia. He went to see this doctor. He was treated. It had been five years since his diagnosis, and he had had no further issues up to that point. He was now married with a child. We were dumbfounded. We were shocked.

Some might say this was coincidental. I would disagree. What are the odds of a couple walking past me at that exact moment whose son had the same diagnosis and who happened to use the same doctor, whose practice was twenty miles away? It was not coincidental. It was God's providential work in my life. That moment was deeply affirming to me. I have rested countless times in the truth that God sent a couple to me the moment I received the news *to encourage me* that he knew this pain would happen to me and it was not surprising. More, he would be present with us during this journey. I still have leukemia. I don't fully know why I have it. I don't know if I will ever know it this side of eternity. It is highly probable, if not certain, that I will have treatment at some point. But I do know the one who has clarity on all those issues. I can trust in him. If he can send someone alongside of me in my most frightening moment to provide encouragement to me, I can trust him for the future and all that it entails. I can be OK with the unknown as long as I know him. It is the truth behind this encounter (of God's undeserved presence, love, and grace) that has enabled me to regularly play, even with leukemia running through my body. In light of this, I want to add to my definition: play is the God-given ability and permission to fully enjoy moments in life as God intended, with freedom and pleasure, *regardless of the circumstances.* God is not God if play is only permissible when life is good. What makes God so powerful, holy, lovely, beautiful, and gracious is that he gives us the ability to play even in the darkest moments of life. It is why I have likely played more in the past ten years than in the previous twenty. It is because I have learned to trust him more intimately because of my cancer than in the absence of it.

BLESSINGS

We often think of what we do not have in life rather than what we do have. Regardless of our circumstances, even in our pain, we are rich if we are in Christ. A psalmist stated, "Then our mouth was filled with laughter, and our tongue with shouts of joy; then they said among the nations, 'The LORD has done great things for them'" (Ps. 126:2). We can laugh because the Lord has done great things for us. He has bestowed on us undeserved and bountiful blessings. God has gifted us with salvation and grace in Christ if we have accepted him. We have meaning and purpose. We have hope in this world and the next. We are truly rich in Christ.

Furthermore, when we laugh and enjoy these rich blessings, it serves as a testimony to God's goodness and our acknowledgment of it. Our confident faith—even while experiencing pain, which typically causes the world to shake its head in bewilderment—will hopefully lead someone to say one day, "The Lord has done great things for them." Perhaps your ability to laugh in the midst of pain will result in someone else turning to Christ.

SUMMARIZING THOUGHTS

It is indeed countercultural to play while experiencing pain. It requires relinquishing control and surrendering completely to the mercy of God. It recognizes that under the authority and goodness of God, pain is never pointless but always has a purpose. Is it excruciatingly hard at times? Yes. Is there a desire to run from it? Yes. Is there a longing for it to be removed immediately and forever? Yes. Are there moments when it is impossible to play because of the depression and despair? Absolutely yes!

But is it also possible to play through and in the pain? Under the authority of God, it is possible. Is it possible to find true freedom and pleasure in play while simultaneously experiencing pain? Within the goodness of God, it is possible. Is it possible to laugh in the moment with genuineness and peace? By looking toward our eventual hope, it is possible. Playing in the midst of pain is a powerful display of our faith in the one who conquered death on the cross, giving us the promise of abundant life, now and forever.

REFLECTION

This chapter is not an easy one to reflect upon. This is in large part because it might lead to more questions than answers. Hope oftentimes does not clarify, but it always assures. As you move toward deeper faith in Christ, I pray you will find the ability to genuinely play with freedom and pleasure, even if the pain persists.

1. Is your pain paralyzing you or moving you closer to Christ? If it is the former, begin to ask Christ to increase your faith.

2. Are you able to affirm that God is good, even if your pain remains? Ask God to reveal his goodness to you in ways that transcend your pain. Be open to redefining goodness.

3. Imagine what your eventual hope looks like in heaven, specifically as it relates to your pain. Allow your imagination to go for a moment, thinking about what awaits you.

4. Begin to memorize the verses in this chapter as a way to internalize the truth that play and pain are not mutually exclusive but can coexist.

5. Are you able to step into play this week? I encourage you to find moments to dance and laugh even in the face of adversity.

EPILOGUE

Learning to Hope: Playing in Glory

> *Joy is the serious business of heaven.*
>
> —C. S. Lewis

Imagine those times when you received great news related to your vocation, relationship, or finances. In that moment, your future felt secure. It might have been when you opened an email to receive a job offer or promotion. The future looked so bright due to employment stability. It might have been the morning after proposing to your fiancée or being proposed to. You now have a companion for life. Or you just crunched the numbers, realizing you have the necessary finances to retire early. In each moment, did you not celebrate? Likely you called your family and friends to share the good news. You booked a reservation at a restaurant so that you could bask in the moment. You looked for every opportunity to show off your engagement ring, even to strangers. You were in the moment, celebrating and enjoying life, because your future seemed secure. But, from our human perspective, the future only *seemed* secure, because our lives could change instantaneously. A recession could cause our company to downsize, thus causing us to lose our dream job. Our fiancé could receive some difficult health news. Or the market could crash, wiping out our retirement plans. We had no guarantee regarding the future, and still, we celebrated.

How much more should we celebrate life knowing that our eternal future *is* secure in Christ. For those in Christ, glory awaits us (1 Cor.

15:50–54). This world is not our home; there is an eternal home awaiting us (John 14:2–3). Our eternal home is perfect without death or sorrow. John described heaven, saying, "He will wipe away every tear from their eyes, and death shall be no more, neither shall there be mourning, nor crying, nor pain anymore, for the former things have passed away" (Rev. 21:4). More than the absence of pain and death, the prize of heaven is the presence of God; "And I heard a loud voice from the throne saying, "Behold, the dwelling place of God is with man. He will dwell with them, and they will be his people, and God himself will be with them as their God" (Rev. 21:3). Perfect communion with God devoid of pain, frustration, and sin awaits each believer in Christ. This is a glorious hope. Should we not celebrate knowing that one day we will inherit a glorious home?

LIFE IN HEAVEN

The Bible provides certain details of life in heaven. We will worship with vibrancy and enthusiasm with individuals from every ethnic group (Rev. 7:9–17). Temptation and sin will be absent, as full sanctification is experienced (Rev. 22:14). Pain will cease to exist, as the impact of the Fall is removed (Rev. 21:4). In other areas, such as the interactions with other people and normal tasks, Scripture is largely silent, which raises numerous questions. What will relationships look like in heaven? Will we have work to do? Will we sleep and exercise? I suspect that one reason details are concealed is that heaven is a far different reality than what we experience on earth or can even fathom. Therefore, it is impossible to fully grasp the new heaven and new earth. It is beyond our comprehension.

PLAY IN HEAVEN

Even though some details are absent in Scripture, we are informed that play will be present in heaven. Zechariah 8 looks forward to a future reality. It states,

> Thus says the LORD: I have returned to Zion and will dwell in the midst of Jerusalem, and Jerusalem shall be called the faithful city, and the mountain of the LORD of hosts, the holy mountain. Thus says the LORD of hosts: Old men and old

women shall again sit in the streets of Jerusalem, each with
staff in hand because of great age. And the streets of the city
shall be full of boys and girls playing in its streets. (vv. 3–5)

Scholars believe the fulfillment of this passage is twofold. It is initially
fulfilled with the restoration of Israel following the Jews' return from
captivity, prior to the birth of Christ. The temple would be rebuilt, and
peace would reign in the land. The ultimate fulfillment occurs with the
second coming of Christ and the establishment of the new heaven and
new earth (Barker 1985, 650). One can speculate whether verse 5 refers
to the intertestamental period or future glory. It is likely pointing to
both periods, similar to Isaiah 7:14, which prophesizes events during
the time of Ahaz as well as the birth of Christ. Thus, Jerusalem would be
restored following its captivity, but a new Jerusalem will also be established in the new heaven. Revelation 21:10–11 states, "And he carried
me away in the Spirit to a great, *high mountain*, and showed me the *holy
city Jerusalem* coming down out of heaven from God, having the glory
of God, its radiance like a most rare jewel, like a jasper, clear as crystal."
The mountain prophesied in Zechariah 8:3 finds ultimate fulfillment in
Revelation 21:10–11.

Yet, the connection between these two passages does not stop with
the mountain. The language of "the streets" is present in both Zechariah
8:4–5 and Revelation 21. Revelation 21:21 describes the streets in the city:
"the street of the city was pure gold, like transparent glass." Zechariah is
foreshadowing this future reality. And based on Zechariah 8:5, we can
anticipate that the "streets of the city shall be full of boys and girls playing
in the streets". Further, the Zechariah passage mirrors Jeremiah when he
prophesied, "Then shall the young women rejoice in the dance, and the
young men and the old shall be merry. I will turn their mourning into
joy; I will comfort them, and give them gladness for sorrow" (Jer. 31:13).
There will be playing in heaven, expressed through dancing.

It makes logical sense. Heaven is a place of perfect freedom without
sin or pain. It involves perfect joy, as we are unrestricted and unhindered
in the presence of God. We will be present in the moment without distraction or anxiety. And, as defined in this book, play is the *God-given*

ability and permission to fully enjoy moments in life as God intended, with freedom and pleasure, regardless of circumstances. If God desires that we fully enjoy life with freedom and pleasure, why would we not experience play in heaven, where perfect freedom is realized upon the removal of sin's bondage and pleasure is no longer tainted by worldly pursuits? In heaven, true play can be experienced in *full freedom and pleasure.*

Pure moments of enjoyment are experienced during play. I want to imagine that heaven will be filled with worshiping God, learning about God, communing with God, and playing in the presence of God. I want to imagine that heaven will consist of robust moments of laughter and enjoyment. I want to imagine that God will celebrate these moments, since he delights in giving us good gifts, in this world and the next. And if this is the reality that awaits us, should we not love life to the fullest as an expression of our eventual but not yet realized heavenly inheritance? Should we not celebrate life in the knowledge that our future is secure? And should we not play now in anticipation of our eventual reality?

Bibliography

Aden, Leroy, and David G. Benner. *Counseling and the Human Predicament: A Study of Sin, Guilt, and Forgiveness.* Ada, MI: Baker, 1989.

Augustine. *The Confessions of St. Augustine.* Translated by John K. Ryan. New York: Image Classics, 1960.

Barclay, William. *The Letters of James and Peter.* Louisville: Westminster John Knox Press, 1961.

Barker, Kenneth L. "Zechariah." In *The Expositors Bible Commentary,* vol. 7, edited by Frank E. Gaebelein, 593–697. Grand Rapids: Zondervan, 1985.

Berk, Laura E. *Exploring Lifespan Development.* Boston: Allyn & Bacon, 2008.

Blackhart, Ginette C., Brian C. Nelson, Roy F. Baumeister, and Megan L. Knowles. "Rejection Elicits Emotional Reactions but Neither Causes Immediate Distress nor Lowers Self-Esteem: A Meta-Analytic Review of 192 Studies on Social Exclusion." *Personality and Social Psychology Review* 13, no. 4 (2009): 269–309.

Brower, Tracey. 2019. "Boost Productivity 20%: The Surprising Power of Play." *Forbes.* March 3, 2019. https://www.forbes.com/sites/tracybrower/2019/03/03/boost-productivity-20-the-surprising-power-of-play/?sh=5e5daba17c05.

Brown, Stuart L. *Play: How It Shapes the Brain, Opens the Imagination, and Invigorates the Soul.* New York: Avery, 2010.

Brown, Stuart L. "Consequences of Play Deprivation." Scholarpedia. 2014. doi:10.4249/scholarpedia.30449.

Cain, Susan. *Quiet: The Power of Introverts in a World That Can't Stop Talking.* New York: Random House, 2012.

Campbell, William S. "Religion, Identity and Ethnicity: The Contribution of Paul the Apostle." *Journal of Beliefs & Values* 29, no. 2 (2008): 39–150.

Cathcart, Rochelle, and Mike Nichols. "Self Theology, Global Theology, and Missional Theology in the Writings of Paul G. Hiebert." *Trinity* 30, no. 2 (2009): 209–221.

Cattanach, Ann. *Play Therapy with Abused Children*. London: Jessica Kingsley, 1993.

Chesterton, G. K. *All Things Considered*. CreateSpace, 2009.

Crimp, Susan. *Katharine Hepburn Once Said . . . : Great Lines to Live By*. New York: HarperCollins, 2003.

Doble, Justin, writer. *The Lord of the Rings: The Rings of Power*. Season 1, episode 5, "Partings." Directed by Wayne Che Yip, featuring Morfydd Clark. Aired September 23, 2022, on Amazon Prime Video.

Dunning, H. Ray. *Grace, Faith, and Holiness: A Wesleyan Systematic Theology*. Kansas City, MO: Beacon Hill, 1988.

Elwell, Walter A., ed. *Evangelical Dictionary of Biblical Theology*. Grand Rapids: Baker, 1996.

Emerson, R. W. *Emerson in His Journals*. Edited by J. Porte. Cambridge, MA: Harvard University Press, 1982.

Erikson, E. H. *Identity, Youth and Crisis*. New York: Norton, 1968.

Erikson, E. H. Obituary. *The New York Times*, May 13, 1994, B9. https://www.nytimes.com/1994/05/13/obituaries/erik-erikson-91-psycho-analyst-who-reshaped-views-of-human-growth-dies.html.

Eschenbacher, Saskia, and Ted Fleming. "Transformative Dimensions of Lifelong Learning: Mezirow, Rorty and COVID-19." *Interview Review of Education* 66 (2020): 657–72.

Frost, Joe L. *A History of Children's Play and Play Environments*. New York: Routledge, 2010.

Fung, Ronald Y. K. *The New International Commentary on the New Testament: The Epistle to the Galatians*. Grand Rapids: Eerdmans, 1988.

Gallagher, J. L. "A Theology of Rest: Sabbath Principles for Ministry," *Saga* 16, no. 1 (2019): 134–49.

Gallup. State of the Global Workforce 2023 Report. https://www.gal-lup.com/workplace/349484/state-of-the-global-workplace.aspx-?thank-you-report-form=1.

Gruber, J., and J. T. Moskowitz. *Positive Emotion: Integrating the Light Sides and Dark Sides.* Oxford: Oxford University Press, 2014.

Hague, Gill. *Understanding Adult Survivors of Domestic Violence in Childhood: Strategies for Recovery for Children and Adults.* London: Jessica Kingsley, 2012.

Hamblin, James. "Buy Experiences, Not Things." *The Atlantic*, October 7, 2014.

Harris, Laird. "Leviticus." In *The Expositors Bible Commentary*, vol. 2, edited by Frank E. Gaebelein, 499–654. Grand Rapids: Zondervan, 1990.

Hiebert, Paul G. "Critical Contextualization." *Missiology* 12, no. 3 (July 1, 1984): 287.

Hiebert, Paul G. "Epistemological Foundations for Science and Theology." *Theological Students Fellowship Bulletin* 8, no. 4 (March–April 1985): 5–10.

Hiebert, Paul G. "Critical Contextualization." *International Bulletin of Missionary Research* 11, no. 3 (July 1, 1987): 4.

Hyun, E. "Making Sense of Developmentally and Culturally Appropriate Practice." In *Early Childhood Education.* New York: Peter Lang, 1998.

Jennings, Willie James. *The Christian Imagination: Theology and the Origin of Race.* New Haven, CT: Yale University Press, 2010.

Johnson, Craig E. *Meeting the Ethical Challenges of Leadership: Casting Light or Shadow.* 7th ed. Newbury Park, CA: Sage, 2021.

Kaiser, Walter. C. Jr. "Exodus." In *The Expositors Bible Commentary*, vol. 2, edited by Frank E. Gaebelein, 285–497. Grand Rapids: Zondervan, 1990.

Keith, M. J., G. Anderson, J. Gaskin, and D. Dean. "Team Video Gaming for Team Building: Effects on Team Performance." *AIS Transactions on Human-Computer Interaction* 10, no. 4 (2018): 205–31.

Kress, Joseph-Anthony. "Eutrapelia: Pleasure for the Soul." *Dominicana.* May 11, 2012. https://www.dominicanajournal.org/eutraplia-plea-sure-for-the-soul/#:~:text=Thomas%20Aquinas%20assigns%20to%20games,soul%20when%20it%20becomes%20overburdened.

Kumar, Amit, Matthew A. Killingsworth, and Thomas Gilovich. "Waiting for Merlot: Anticipatory Consumption of Experiential and Material Purchases." *Psychological Science*, August 21, 2014.

Lewis, C. S. *The Problem of Pain*. 1940. San Francisco: HarperCollins, 2001.

Lewis, C. S. *The Weight of Glory*. 1949. San Francisco: HarperCollins, 2001.

Lewis, C. S. *Letters to Malcolm: Chiefly on Prayer*. 1964. Boston: Mariner, 2002.

Li, Guofang. "Immigrant Children's Play Can Clash with Mainstream Culture." The Conversation. August 9, 2017. https://theconversation.com/immigrant-childrens-play-can-clash-with-mainstream-cultures-81927#:~:text=Play%20is%20part%20of%20the,language%2C%20context%20and%20social%20norms.

Liu, Richard T. "Childhood Maltreatment and Impulsivity: A Meta-Analysis and Recommendations for Future Study." *Journal of Abnormal Child Psychology* 47 (2019): 221–43.

Narvaez, Darcia, Jaak Panksepp, Allan N. Schore, and Tracy R. Gleason, eds. *Evolution, Early Experience and Human Development: From Research to Practice and Policy*. Oxford: Oxford University Press, 2012.

Nolland, John. *The New International Greek Testament Commentary: The Gospel of Matthew*. Grand Rapids: Eerdmans, 2005.

O'Brien, Peter T. *Colossians, Philemon*. Word Biblical Commentary. Grand Rapids: Zondervan, 1982.

Panksepp, Jaak, and Lucy Biven. *The Archaeology of Mind: Neuroevolutionary Origins of Human Emotions*. New York: Norton, 2013.

Patterson, Serena J., Ingrid Sochting, and James E. Marcia. "The Inner Space and Beyond: Women and Identity." In *Adolescent Identity Formation*, edited by Gerald R. Adams, Thomas P. Gullotta, and Raymond Montemayor, 9–24. Newbury Park, CA: Sage, 1992.

Piaget, J. *Play, Dreams and Imitation in Childhood*. New York: Routledge, 2013.

Potkay, Adam. "Spenser, Donne, and the Theology of Joy." *Studies in English Literature, 1500–1900* 46, no. 1 (2006): 43–66.